Discover! Social Studies

4

Discover! Social Studies 4B

Published in Catasauqua, Pennsylvania by Discover Press, a division of Edovate Learning Corp.

334 2nd Street

Catasauqua, PA 18032

edovate.com

ISBN: 978-1-956330-10-6

Printed in United States of America

1st Edition

Table of Contents

Worktexts & Instructor Guides

Worktexts

- Your Discover! course integrates all reading, writing, practice, ideas to extend learning, and opportunities for students to capture their ideas and connect learning to what matters to them.
- By providing both direct instruction and assessment opportunities, students are able to gain knowledge, reflect on what they learned, and apply it in both academic and real-world environments.
- To meet the needs of all learners, each worktext includes activities, instruction, and extensions that appeal to all learning styles.
- Each chapter is made up of lessons that connect to a central theme. Students have the opportunity to demonstrate understanding and think critically as they move through each lesson, and each chapter culminates with a student review, assessment, and opportunities for students to show what they know.

Instructor Guides

- Each instructor guide is specifically constructed to complement the worktext, provide helpful suggestions for a home-based instructor, offer support, and broaden a student's knowledge base.
- Instruction and curriculum are differentiated with remediation, enrichment, assessment, and supporting activities suitable for a variety of learning styles.
- Answer keys for all activities are included in your instructor guide.

Planning Your Day & School Year

- Each lesson takes approximately two to three days to complete, for a total of around 150 days of instruction through the school year. NOTE: Your worktext and instructor guide provide enrichment activities and discussion questions to take learning further and may add extra days to the school year. These are designed to inspire the instructor to customize the learning experience even further and encourage students to dive deeper into the topic.
- As you begin each lesson, we recommend completing three pages on the first day and two pages, including Show What You Know, on the second day.
- In the chapter reviews and assessment lessons, we recommend completing three pages on the first day and the remaining pages on the second day.

Parts of a Lesson

Lesson Overview (PAGE 1):

Each lesson opens with a list of goals or objectives designed to set the student up for success. Your instructor guide provides additional resources to reinforce concepts and add creativity to the lesson.

Explore (PAGE 2):

This page is key, as it is designed to engage students and encourage the discovery of new concepts.

Direct Instruction (PAGES 3–5):

In this section, the student gets to work by reading the content, capturing their own thoughts and ideas, and then practicing the concepts:

- **Read**: Students read informational text to gain knowledge about the lesson topic.
- **Write**: Students reflect on what they have read by creating a written response.
- **Practice**: Students practice what they have learned through various engaging activities, such as graphic organizers, matching, drawing, experiments, and hands-on learning.

Show What You Know (PAGE 6):

This is where students demonstrate what they've learned by completing a carefully crafted assessment aligned with the lesson's objectives.

To reinforce learning, additional extension activities are included throughout each lesson:

- **Create**: Students are tasked with constructing a piece of art, such as a drawing, song, poem, model, etc., to demonstrate learning.
- **Take a Closer Look**: With these activities, students make observations about the world around them. In doing so, students are able to generate predictions, inferences, or conclusions based on those observations. In science, these are scientific investigations or STEM-based activities.
- **In the Real World**: These activities connect the lesson to real-world situations. Students get the opportunity to investigate or interact with real-world examples.
- **Online Connection**: Students use technology-based solutions to research and investigate concepts related to the lesson or create artifacts demonstrating their understanding.
- **Play**: In these activities, students create or play games related to the lesson, such as board games, card games, role-playing, etc.

Chapter 6

National Growth and Conflict

Hi, my friend! It is Monty, the hug-loving lion!

The last time we talked, we learned about how the United States expanded westward. I wanted to see all of it!

I asked Professor Tibbs when we would catch our flight to the West. He said, "If you want to learn what it was like when the United States expanded, you have to travel as they did." I thought and said, "You mean by horse? Horses don't like lions! They run away." He laughed and said, "No! We will go by train."

So we left Boston and started on our way. We passed through the states of New York and Pennsylvania. Maria said, "This country is so beautiful!" I couldn't agree more.

After two days of riding, we entered the state of Missouri. I asked Professor Tibbs when this beautiful territory became a state. He answered, "In 1820, but it has a sad history."

"Oh no," Maria said. We both asked why. "When this territory became a state, they allowed people to keep slaves," said Professor Tibbs.

I shook my head sadly. I thought to myself that I need to learn from the history of America. Then when I go back to the savanna, I will make sure everyone is free.

What Will I Learn?

This chapter examines the expansion of the United States westward in the period following the War of 1812. It focuses on important milestones such as the Monroe Doctrine and Missouri Compromise.

Lessons at a Glance

Lesson 37

War of 1812

By the end of this lesson, you will be able to:

- identify the reasons for the War of 1812
- analyze the reasons that the United States and Great Britain were not prepared to enter into another war
- identify the similarities and differences of the navies from the United States and Great Britain during the War of 1812

Lesson Review

If you need to review the relationship between America and Great Britain and why the United States declared its independence from Great Britain, please go to the lesson titled "Tensions."

Academic Vocabulary

Read the following vocabulary words and definitions. Look through the lesson. Can you find each vocabulary word? Underline the vocabulary word in your lesson. Write the page number of where you found each word in the blanks.

- **alliance:** an agreement between two groups to help each other (page ___)
- **chief:** the leader of a tribe or group of people (page ___)
- **colony:** a place in a different country where a group of people move to start new lives while staying connected to their home country (page ___)
- **deserter:** a person who has fled military service (page ___)
- **expansion:** the settling of land beyond the borders of a country (page ___)
- **frontier:** land beyond the border of the country (page ___)
- **impressment:** being taken against your will to fight for another country (page ___)
- **merchant vessel:** a ship carrying goods for trade (page ___)
- **navy:** a branch of the military that fights at sea (page ___)
- **trade:** the action of exchanging something for something else (page ___)
- **treaties:** agreements between countries or people (page ___)

CREE

A treaty is an agreement made between countries or people. The goal of a treaty is to reach a peaceful decision that satisfies both groups. Think about an argument you had with a family member or friend. Disagreements cause problems, or conflict, so you will create a treaty, an agreement. Meet with the person you disagreed with. Work together to come up with a solution to your problem that you both feel is fair. Give your treaty a title. Use complete sentences to fully explain the solution to your problem on your paper. Make sure you and the other person sign the treaty. Place your treaty somewhere you can see it.

EXPLRE

Imagine you are an American sailor on a ship in the year 1807. You are sailing across the Atlantic Ocean toward Spain. You depend on the wind to fill your ship's sails each day and take you across the sea. Your cargo, or goods you carry, includes cotton and tobacco.

Suddenly you see another ship in the distance. Whipping in the wind, you see the British flag flying above the ship's sails. You hear a loud booming sound and realize the British ship has fired a cannon toward you. The crew of your ship suddenly jumps into action. Men grab rifles and daggers. But your captain knows your ship is prepared for **trade**, or exchanging goods for resources or currency, not war with the most powerful navy in the world.

Soon British officers have boarded your vessel, and your shipmates are unarmed and standing in a line. One by one, the sailors are asked to explain their business on board. Four men are pushed forward and forced onto the naval ship. They are never seen again.

What could the British navy want with your sailors? How do you feel after the terrifying experience? How do you expect your country's government to react?

....

....

....

....

....

....

....

....

....

TAKE A CLOSER LOOK

From 1803 to 1815, Great Britain was fighting in the Napoleonic Wars against France. They hoped to disrupt American trade with France and struggled to find enough men to serve in their navy, the branch of the military that fights at sea. Great Britain resorted to impressment, forcing some foreign sailors into its armed services. This caused the United States to consider another war with Great Britain.

READ

US Expansion

In 1800, the United States sought **expansion**, or the settling of land beyond its borders. It also sought success in trade with other nations. Expansion would bring the United States more resources, and trade would bring profit from selling them. The United States wished to become prosperous. Conflicts with Great Britain complicated these goals.

Great Britain and France were at war. Great Britain did not want America to trade with its enemy. Great Britain forced American trading ships to stop in British ports to pay taxes.

The British also boarded American **merchant vessels**, trade ships carrying goods. They sought **deserters**, or men who had fled service in the British military. Some US sailors were forced onto British ships to help Great Britain's **navy** fight against France. This was called **impressment**.

In 1807, the British Royal Navy fired on the US ship Chesapeake and took four sailors. President Jefferson signed the Embargo Act, which stopped trade with Great Britain. This hurt the US shipping industry and angered many eastern states.

Canada also had problems. Canada had many British **colonies**, areas of land controlled by Great Britain. As Americans moved west, they took control of lands in the **frontier**, or land beyond the border of the country. Native Americans and British colonists in Canada were concerned the United States would take their lands.

TAKE A CLOSER LOOK

Tecumseh, the Native American chief of the Shawnee tribe, was determined to protect his language and way of life. Both his father and brother were killed in the late 1700s as US troops took control of his tribal lands. He inspired Native Americans to continue to fight for their culture and homelands. He felt creating an alliance with Great Britain might give Native Americans the opportunity to prevent further US expansion.

Conflicts at Home and Sea

The **chief** of the Shawnees, Tecumseh, spoke to leaders of other Native American tribes. He wanted to join forces, create one nation, and put a stop to westward expansion. He asked them to stop signing over land to the United States in **treaties**. This caused conflicts between American settlers and Native Americans to increase.

Americans thought Great Britain had formed an **alliance**, an agreement between two groups to help each other, with Tecumseh and his people. Americans accused the British of providing food and weapons to Native American tribes.

When James Madison became president in 1809, tension continued to rise between Great Britain and the United States. Both nations had reasons to avoid a war. Great Britain had just lost a war to the United States, was already fighting another war against France, and needed more sailors. Any fighting on United States or North American soil gave America an advantage.

The United States worried that Great Britain might win a war. The US ships were stronger and faster, but they only had 16 of them. Great Britain's navy had 500. Also, many Americans did not want to start another war. The northeastern states wanted to focus on trade and improving the country's military.

James Madison was the fourth president of the United States. He declared war with Great Britain in 1812, but many states did not support his decision. Massachusetts, Rhode Island, and Connecticut refused to send troops to fight when asked. They felt the war was not necessary, that trade restrictions had hurt the shipping industry, and that the US military was not prepared.

Do you agree with Madison's decision? If you were president, would you have declared war with Great Britain in 1812? Explain why or why not.

What reasons did the United States have for getting involved in another war with Great Britain?

Considering War

Foreseeing a war, Major General Sir Isaac Brock, the British commander in Canada, began enlisting Native Americans to increase the size of the Canadian armed forces. In 1811, William Henry Harrison, governor of Indiana's territory, attacked and destroyed Prophetstown, the Native American settlement led by Tecumseh at the Battle of Tippecanoe. Tecumseh decided to join General Brock with a group of Native American warriors.

Congressmen dedicated to westward expansion used the unrest between Native Americans and citizens on the frontier to encourage war with Great Britain. These politicians were called war hawks. Insisting a war fought against Great Britain but in its Canadian colonies would ensure a victory, President James Madison signed a declaration of war on June 18, 1812.

WRITE

Would you rather be a member of the British Royal Navy or the United States Navy in the 1800s? Explain your thinking on the lines below.

Why was the United States hesitant about declaring war with Great Britain? Who did the United States seem to be underestimating?

PRACTICE

Imagine you are President Madison. You must decide whether or not to go to war with Great Britain in 1812. What are some reasons to engage in a new war? Write your ideas in the "Pros" column. What are your reasons to avoid war? Write your ideas in the "Cons" column.

PROS	CONS

REVIEW

In this lesson, you learned:

- After the Revolutionary War, Great Britain sought to stop US trade.
- Great Britain impressed, or forced, American sailors into British naval service.
- Native Americans joined British military forces in Canada to stop US expansion.
- Great Britain's navy was the largest and most powerful in the world.
- The US navy was small, but its ships were strong and fast.
- Great Britain was at war with France from 1803 to 1815.
- President Madison declared war with Great Britain in 1812.

Think About It

The United States began the war of 1812 without a large, strong military. Are there other methods of solving disputes you would recommend to President Madison?

Circle the correct answer for each question.

1. The British Royal Navy was _______.
   A. large and powerful
   B. small and weak
   C. small but fast
   D. large but weak

2. The US Navy had _______.
   A. 500 ships
   B. 16 ships
   C. 100 ships
   D. 5 ships

3. True or False   Great Britain did not want to begin another war with the United States because they were at war with Germany.

Answer the following question with complete sentences.

4. Describe one reason the United States went to war with Great Britain in 1812.

....

....

....

....

....

ONLINE CONNECTION

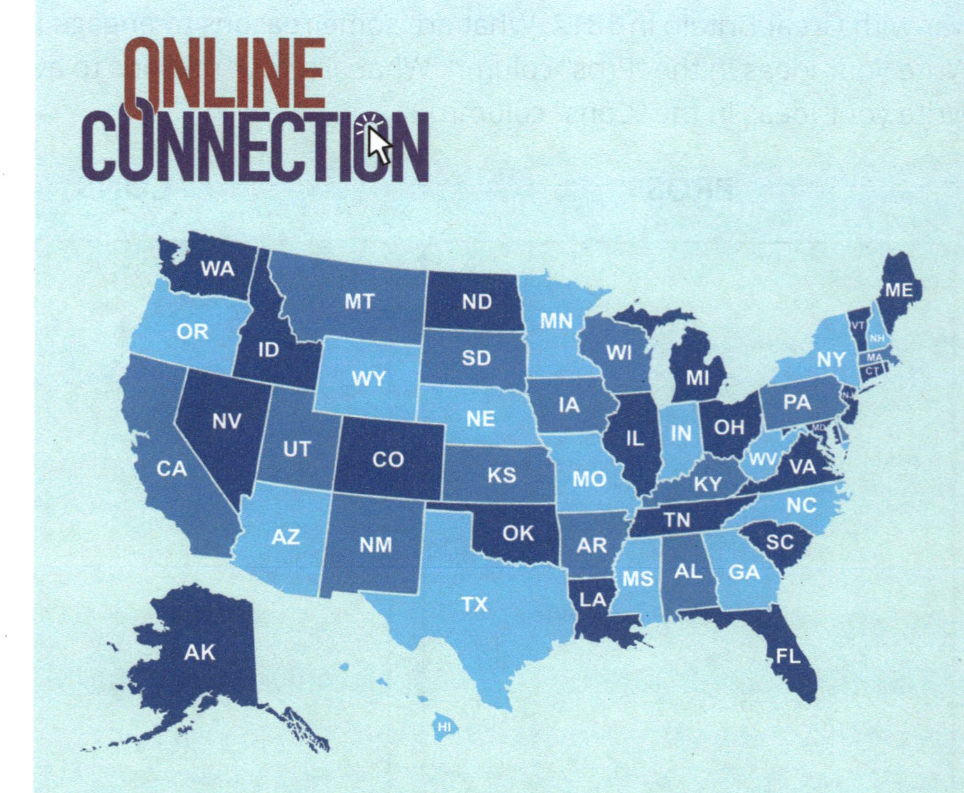

Look at the map of the United States. Then find a map online of the United States in 1812. How are the maps different? What goal was the United States trying to achieve? Write your answers below.

....

....

....

Lesson 38

Results of the War of 1812

By the end of this lesson, you will be able to:

- identify why the Battle of New Orleans occurred despite a treaty being in place between the United States and Great Britain
- evaluate how the War of 1812 affected America
- describe American military engagements in Canada that did not succeed
- explain how Americans showed patriotism, including Francis Scott Key and Dolley Madison

Lesson Review

If you need to review the causes of the War of 1812, please go to the lesson titled "War of 1812."

Academic Vocabulary

Read the following vocabulary words and definitions. Look through the lesson. Can you find each vocabulary word? Underline the vocabulary word in your lesson. Write the page number of where you found each word in the blanks.

- **frigates:** naval warships (page ___)
- **Indigenous:** native to a particular region (page ___)
- **national anthem:** a song chosen to inspire a country's people (page ___)
- **patriotism:** a demonstration of pride in one's country (page ___)
- **Treaty of Ghent:** the treaty between the United States and Great Britain that ended the War of 1812 (page ___)
- **war hawks:** congressmen who supported the War of 1812 and westward expansion (page ___)
- **Washington, DC:** the capital of the United States (page ___)

CRETE

What do you love most about your country? Perhaps you love a particular place, one of your country's heroes, or a freedom your country's government protects.

Create a patriotic collage showing all of the things you love most about your country. A collage is a piece of artwork made of many illustrations, photographs, magazine clippings, or fabric. You can begin to make a patriotic collage by finding a large piece of paper or cardboard. Glue drawings, pictures, or images from magazines. Print photographs you find online, or photocopy your own family photographs to add to your collage.

The War of 1812 inspired many citizens to love their country and be patriotic. Francis Scott Key wrote "The Star Spangled Banner," a poem inspired by what he observed during the War of 1812. His poem was turned into a song and became the United States' national anthem.

Patriotism is a demonstration of love for one's country. Singing a national anthem, flying your country's flag, and celebrating national holidays are all ways to show patriotism. Read the first lines of "The Star Spangled Banner" written below:

O say, can you see, by the dawn's early light,
What so proudly we hailed at the twilight's last gleaming
Whose broad stripes and bright stars through the perilous fight,
O'er the ramparts we watched were so gallantly streaming?
And the rocket's red glare, the bombs bursting in air,
Gave proof through the night that our flag was still there,
O say, does that star-spangled banner yet wave
O'er the land of the free and the home of the brave?

What words from this poem show Francis Scott Key's patriotism? Does it surprise you that a war inspired these feelings in Francis Scott Key?

....

....

....

....

Francis Scott Key

Francis Scott Key watched as soldiers raised an American flag following a long battle in Baltimore, Maryland. The battle took place in 1814, long into the War of 1812. Can you make a prediction about the war based on his poem? Do you think the United States was victorious?

READ

Expectations of Victory

After the Revolutionary War, America tried to expand westward and build a strong economy by trading with Europe and Asia. Great Britain responded by limiting American trade with Great Britain and other European nations. Great Britain also used impressment to build up its navy by capturing American sailors and forcing them to work on naval **frigates**, or warships, in their war against France.

Supported by **war hawks**, congressmen in favor of US expansion, President Madison declared war against Great Britain on June 18, 1812. The United States tried to capture the Lake Ontario region, including the Niagara River. This allowed the United States to control a transportation route in Canada and continue their invasion. The United States expected an easy victory, but the forces of Major General Brock and Tecumseh met them with strong resistance.

The Canadian and Native American forces pushed American troops back into US territory and seized Detroit. In October of 1812, American troops crossed into Canada from New York to take more territory by the Niagara River. The Canadian forces won again, but Major General Brock was killed.

The Americans and British continued to battle near Lake Ontario and Lake Erie. In September 1813, the United States took control of Lake Erie. In October 1813, Tecumseh was killed in the Battle of the Thames.

WRITE

How did battles with British colonists in Canada surprise the US forces?

....

....

....

TAKE A CLOSER LOOK

The Great Lakes

Lake Ontario and Lake Erie were sites of much of the conflict between Canada and the United States during the War of 1812. If the United States could control this region, they could control the movement of ships and supplies and continue their invasion into Canada. Throughout the war, the United States had victories and did gain control of Lake Erie but did not make much progress. Even today, these lakes mark the border between Canada and the United States.

READ

Treaties and Patriotism

Most of Great Britain's naval forces were busy fighting the French. In 1814, it was clear the British had won. They sent their warships to line the United States' east coast. On August 24, 1814, the British navy landed in Chesapeake Bay and stormed **Washington, D.C.,** the US capital. They burned the White House and much of the city. James Madison's wife, Dolley Madison, saved important documents and a famous portrait of George Washington from the flames.

On September 11, 1814, the US navy won the Battle of Plattsburgh in New York and brought hope for a US victory in the war. Fighting at Fort McHenry in Baltimore, Maryland, had a similar effect. When the fighting ceased at Fort McHenry, soldiers raised a large American flag. This supposedly inspired Francis Scott Key to write "The Star-Spangled Banner." This song later became the US **national anthem**, a song chosen to inspire a country's people.

These battles led to the beginning of peace talks in Ghent, Belgium, between Great Britain and the United States. A treaty for peace, the **Treaty of Ghent**, was signed by both countries on December 24, 1814. Sadly, news that the war had ended did not reach all of the American or British troops for some time. British ships attacked New Orleans on January 8, 1815. Major General Andrew Jackson became a hero by leading a defense of the city. Jackson would later become President of the United States.

Andrew Jackson

TAKE A CLOSER LOOK

A Hero to the People

For his efforts during the War of 1812, especially during the Battle of New Orleans, Andrew Jackson was called an American hero. As president, Andrew Jackson removed the remaining Native American tribes from their lands in the southeast, and forcing them to march thousands of miles west, in what became known as the Trail of Tears. Many Native Americans died on this march. Today, Andrew Jackson's portrait is found on the US $20 bill.

Some people feel his actions as president do not earn him a place on US currency. A new $20 bill is being designed with Harriet Tubman's portrait. Do you think Andrew Jackson's portrait should be removed from the US $20 bill?

READ

US Victory

When the fighting was finally over, it was clear the War of 1812 affected the country in multiple ways. It led to feelings of patriotism in the United States. Stories of Andrew Jackson's bravery, Dolly Madison's dedication, and the words of "The Star-Spangled Banner" created unity. Citizens were proud of their young country's ability to defend itself against Great Britain once again.

Signing the Treaty of Ghent also helped create some stability for the US, bringing peace between Great Britain and America. While it did not punish Great Britain's use of impressment, it did create a clear boundary between Canada and the US. Westward expansion would continue without interference from Great Britain.

However, Native American hopes for a nation of **Indigenous**, or native, people were now over. With Tecumseh's death, the alliance between the Native American tribes and Great Britain was at an end. Settlers would continue to move west.

WRITE

Do you feel the Treaty of Ghent was fair? What would you add to the treaty?

....

....

....

....

....

REVIEW

In this lesson, you learned:

- America attacked the Canadian border, starting the War of 1812. The strength of Canadian troops aided by Native Americans surprised the US troops.
- The war increased American patriotism and continued westward expansion.
- The Battle of New Orleans occurred after the Treaty of Ghent was signed because the British navy was not aware of the treaty.

Think About It

Who do you feel demonstrated patriotism? Do you feel any British figures or allies were heroic? Can you disagree with the goals or decisions your country has made in the past and still remain patriotic?

PRACTICE

How did the alliance between the British forces of Canada and Native American warriors impact battles between America and Canada?

Describe at least one result of the War of 1812.

How did each important figure demonstrate patriotism?

Patriot	Proof of Patriotism
Dolley Madison	
Francis Scott Key	
Andrew Jackson	

1. Circle all of the results of the War of 1812.

   A. Great Britain paid America for its use of impressment.

   B. Great Britain agreed to end opposition to American westward expansion.

   C. Borders between Canada and the U.S. were drawn.

   D. Patriotism and unity increased in the United States.

   E. Lands were returned to Native Americans.

2. Why did the Battle of New Orleans take place after the Treaty of Ghent was signed?

   A. Great Britain was trying to play a trick on the United States.

   B. Some British troops did not know the war was over.

   C. Some American officers did not agree with the treaty.

   D. America had declared war again.

3. What did Dolley Madison, Andrew Jackson, and Francis Scott Key have in common after the war?

4. True or False America was able to invade and conquer most of Great Britain's colonies during the War of 1812.

Weapons of the War of 1812

Warfare in 1812 was very different from modern-day warfare. Troops marched on foot, moving slowly. Weapons and clothing were heavy. The United States and Great Britain used cannons, rifles, muskets, bayonets, and swords during their battles. Guns were fired from long distances toward the enemy.

How do you think the weapons and supplies carried in the 1800s created challenges for men in the British and American armies?

Lesson 39

Monroe Doctrine and Missouri Compromise

By the end of this lesson, you will be able to:

- summarize the viewpoints of opposing sides of the debate that resulted in the Missouri Compromise
- describe the main principles of the Monroe Doctrine

Lesson Review

If you need to review Louisiana Territory and expansion, please go to the lesson titled "Louisiana Territory."

Academic Vocabulary

Read the following vocabulary words and definitions. Look through the lesson. Can you find each vocabulary word? Underline the vocabulary word in your lesson. Write the page number of where you found each word in the blanks.

- **colonization:** when one country takes control of another country or region, establishing a settlement (page ____)
- **Western Hemisphere:** the side of the earth including North and South America (page ____)

James Monroe

On a spring day in April of 1758, James Monroe was born. James Monroe was not only the fifth president, but he was also a founding father of the United States. James Monroe's presidency was influential in setting the foundation for US foreign policy. He implemented the Monroe Doctrine. This doctrine would be a key in US foreign policy.

Monroe served as president for eight years. His time as president is important because of the Missouri Compromise of 1820 and the Monroe Doctrine.

EXPLORE

The United States was divided by the issue of slavery in the 1817 when Monroe became president. In general, the 11 Southern states felt states should have the power to decide whether slavery was allowed. Most people in the 11 Northern states felt slavery should stop. When the Missouri Territory wanted to enter the United States as a slave state, the balance of power would tip toward the pro-slavery group.

All the politicians arguing the slavery issue were free men. The enslaved people had no voice in the discussion. Their freedom was in the hands of the US government. As you look back at history, it is important to think about whether the people before you did the right thing or the wrong thing.

Do you think it was right or wrong to allow Missouri to enter the Union as a slave state?

....

....

....

....

....

....

TAKE A CLOSER LOOK

When Thomas Jefferson purchased the Louisiana Territory from France in 1803, it doubled the size of the United States. People started to settle in the West. This land was divided into territories, which were able to apply to be a state when enough settlers had moved there. The issue of slavery in the new territories was a topic of debate from the very beginning.

Modern map of the US Louisiana Purchase territory (in dark brown)

The Missouri Compromise

Missouri applied for statehood in 1818, and many in the territory wanted to allow slavery. The United States was divided at the time into anti-slavery and pro-slavery. People wanted there to be a balance between slave and free states. This led to the Missouri Compromise. The Missouri Compromise of 1820 was an agreement made to keep the balance of slave and free states equal. Missouri became a part of the United States as a slave state in 1820, and Maine joined as a free state in 1821. The compromise also made a decision about slavery in the remaining territories of the Louisiana Purchase. Slavery was banned above the 36°30′ parallel and allowed below that line.

Southerners opposed the Missouri Compromise because it set an example for Congress to make laws about slavery. They argued that states should decide to enter the Union as a slave state or a free state. Northerners disliked the law because it meant slavery was expanded into new territory.

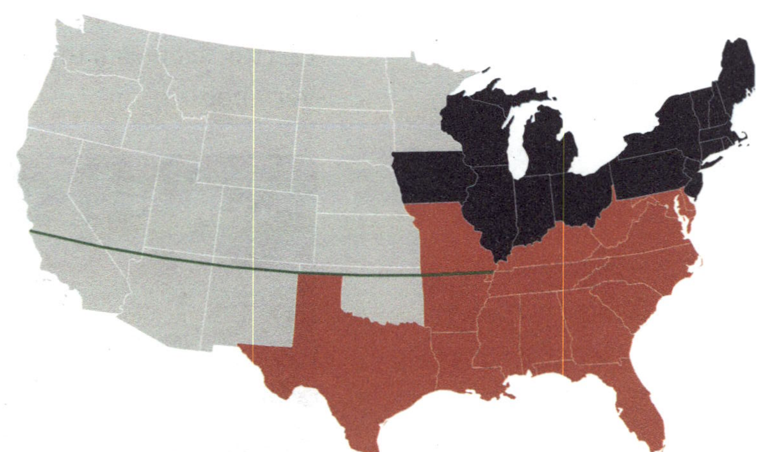

Map of the United States in 1849, with the parallel 36°30' north—slave states in red, free states in blue.

Why Did the Missouri Compromise Fail?

The Missouri Compromise was ineffective because it did not deal with the issue of slavery in all the states. The question remained: whether to allow slavery or not in both the existing states and in the territories. More compromises occurred to try to keep the balance until the answer was decided by the Civil War.

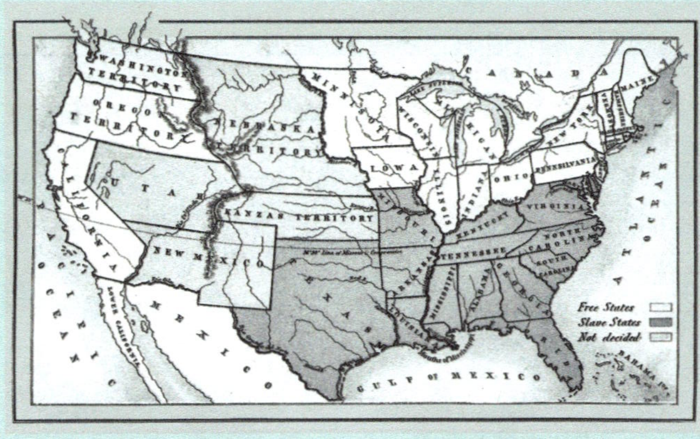

Map of free, slave, and undecided states in 1857

What was the view of slave states on the Missouri Compromise?

READ

Revolution Spreads

After the success of the American Revolution, the French people also revolted against their king in 1789. This upset the colonial powers of Europe to the point that many of the colonies in Central and South America also had successful revolutions. When things settled down in European politics, President Monroe was afraid that the Europeans would try to reclaim their colonies. This would weaken US power in the **Western Hemisphere**, which includes all the land of North and South America and the Caribbean Islands.

THE MONROE DOCTRINE

In 1823, President James Monroe declared that North and South America were no longer open to **colonization**. In other words, the doctrine stated that European nations could not interfere with independent governments in the Western Hemisphere, and the United States would not get involved in European affairs, including those colonies already existing in the Americas. If a European power tried to interfere with any nation in the Americas, the United States would view it as a hostile action.

Countries in the Western Hemisphere

Prospects of war with the United States probably helped keep European powers from trying to reconquer the newly independent nations in the Western Hemisphere. France tried to retake Mexico in 1862 while the United States was distracted by the Civil War, but they left in 1867 when the United States was able to send troops.

The Four Main Purposes of the Monroe Doctrine

1. European countries would not interfere with the Americas and would not colonize it further.
2. The United States would recognize and not interfere with existing colonies in the Americas.
3. The United States would not interfere with European affairs.
4. Any interference from Europe would be viewed as hostile by the United States.

PRACTICE

Using the facts about the Monroe Doctrine and the Missouri Compromise of 1820 listed below, fill out the chart. Be sure to put the correct fact below either the Monroe Doctrine or Missouri Compromise.

- Closed colonization of the Americas to Europe
- Declared Europe cannot interfere with affairs in the Americas
- Maine entered the United States as a free state
- It was a way to keep the balance between free states and slave states
- Declared if Europe interfered with any countries of the Americas, the United States would view it as a hostile action
- Did not address the question of if slavery would continue in the United States
- The United States would recognize colonies of Europe already established in the Americas

Monroe Doctrine	Missouri Compromise

In this lesson, you learned:

- The Missouri Compromise tried and failed to address the issue of slavery.
- The Monroe Doctrine said the United States would defend other nations in the Western Hemisphere from European colonization.

Think About It

Why was the Monroe Doctrine important for US foreign policy?

SHOW WHAT YOU KNOW

Circle the correct answer.

1. Who implemented the Monroe Doctrine?

A. Thomas Jefferson

B. James Monroe

C. George Washington

D. Theodore Roosevelt

2. What was the compromise made in the Missouri Compromise?

A. Maine would enter the Union as a slave state and Missouri would enter as a free state

B. Maine would enter the Union as a free state and Missouri would enter as a slave state

C. Maine and Missouri would both enter the Union as free states

D. Maine and Missouri would both enter the Union as slave states

3. What is colonization?

A. to visit a new place

B. to explore and learn about a new region or country

C. when one country takes control of another country or region

D. to relocate a city to a new place

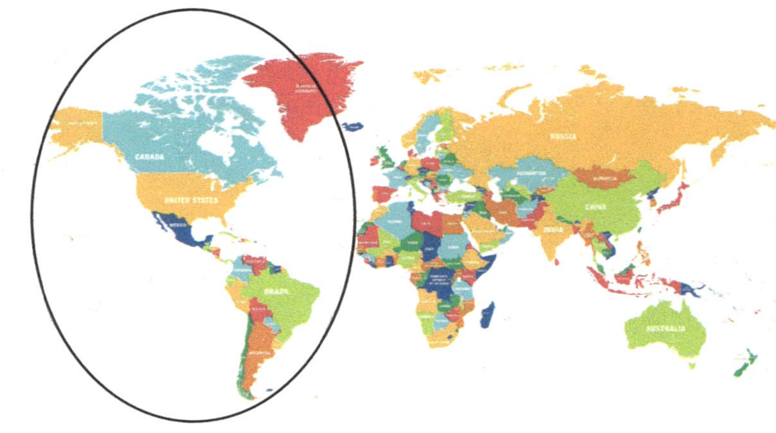

4. True or False The area circled on the map to the right is the Western Hemisphere.

5. True or False The Missouri Compromise brought the country together.

6. What were the four main points in the Monroe Doctrine?

....

....

....

7. Why did Southern states disagree with the Missouri Compromise?

8. Why did Northern states disagree with the Missouri Compromise?

Create a poster that illustrates the four main concepts of the Monroe Doctrine. In your own words, write each of the main ideas of the Monroe Doctrine and draw a picture to help understand the concept. Here is an example for the first concept: "European countries would not interfere with the Americas and would not colonize it further."

Lesson 40

Transportation

By the end of this lesson, you will be able to:

- explain how communities benefited from developments in canals, steamboats, roads, and the postal system
- describe how the railroad was important to the growth and development of the United States
- describe how factories developed across New England

Lesson Review

If you need to review the effects of the War of 1812 on the United States, please go to the lesson titled "Results of the War of 1812."

Academic Vocabulary

Read the following vocabulary words and definitions. Look through the lesson. Can you find each vocabulary word? Underline the vocabulary word in your lesson. Write the page number of where you found each word in the blanks.

- **canal:** a channel of water made by humans for boat transportation or for bringing water to crops (page ____)
- **industrialization:** a process where countries begin to use machines to do work (page ____)
- **steamboats:** boats propelled by steam engines (page ____)
- **watermill:** a water wheel connected to a device that drives a mechanical process (page ____)

After the War of 1812, patriotism grew. The US victory led to unity in the United States. The need for connection led to the construction of the transcontinental railroad, canals, and roads throughout the country. Additionally, more links to communities allowed for more accessible transport of raw materials. The United States now had more effective ways to transport materials, which led to the development of factories in New England.

EXPLORE

When people started settling west, they used carts pulled by oxen. This mode of transportation was long and dangerous. As the United States grew, communities needed to be connected. In 1800, Thomas Jefferson was elected as the third US president. Jefferson wanted to discover a waterway that crossed from the Atlantic Ocean to the Pacific and build a system of trade that connected people throughout the country. By the mid-1800s, there were dirt roads throughout parts of the United States, river steamboats increased, and boats traveled along manufactured canals.

Workers finished the first coast-to-coast railroad in 1869. Towns and cities could develop farther away from major waterways. Small communities built links to the railroad system. Jefferson's wish to connect people throughout the nation was a reality.

Why is it important that communities in the United States are connected?

....

....

What design helped connect the United States?

....

....

....

Carts pulled by oxen were one of the first ways people moved west.

The transcontinental railroad connected the West and East Coast.

Think About It

How do you travel today? Many places still use trains to travel. Some trains now travel underground and are called subways. Other ways people travel are planes and cars. What transportation do you use most? If you were to travel across the United States, what mode of transport would you use?

Transportation is a key tool to connecting the nation and the world.

READ

Developments and Benefits of Canals, Steamboats, and Roads

As the United States grew, methods of travel and ways to provide for a community did as well. More land was being farmed, which called for water. People traveled farther, so the need for roads and boat travel increased.

Canals are channels of water made by humans for boat transportation or for bringing water to crops. Communities benefited from canals as they allowed farmers a cheaper way to get their goods to markets. Canals provide waterway shortcuts from one region to another. An example of a canal is the Erie Canal, which opened up trade in the Midwest. Opening up trade in the Midwest boosted economic development in the area.

Steamboats are boats propelled by steam engines. Steamboats used rivers such as the Mississippi for transporting goods and travel. Steamboats changed transportation in the United States by providing easy travel upriver. They cut travel times in half.

In 1811, construction began on Cumberland Road, a national highway that provided a route from Maryland to Illinois. The development of Cumberland Road and the government funding other roads led to more expansion westward. The creation of transportation infrastructure benefited settlers and farmers, letting them travel more effectively.

Erie Canal in 1906

Steamboat

WRITE

What was one benefit of steamboats?

The Railroad

The desire to move west and transport goods from the West led to railroad development. Before the railroad, people used wagons pulled by horses and oxen. Traveling this way was dangerous and took a long time. The construction of the railroad allowed more people to settle and travel west. The United States grew economically by transporting raw materials from the West to factories in the East. Also, it connected people in the West and the East.

THE POSTAL SERVICE

With roads, canals, and the railroad, the postal service became more practical. The completion of the transcontinental railroad in 1869 connected the West and the East. People could send letters from one side of the nation to the other. The US Postal Service is a public service, meaning they do not need to break even. This keeps prices low so more people can use the service.

NEW ENGLAND FACTORIES

In New England, industrialization began along rivers. **Industrialization** is a process where countries begin to use machines to do work. After the War of 1812, industrialization expanded as roads, canals, railroads, and steamboats made raw goods available in the West.

Watermills were created in New England's many rivers. A **watermill** is a water wheel connected to a device that drives a mechanical process. Watermills grind agricultural produce, cut lumber, and shape metal. New England's large population allowed for more manufacturing jobs and factories.

Indigenous People and the Railroad

The railroad cut across Indigenous lands, and more people settled there. This affected Indigenous people's way of life. Tribes resisted the construction of the railroad, but their efforts were overpowered. Many tribes were relocated to reservations to make way for the railroad.

Name two effects of the railroad.

1. ....

2. ....

READ

Effects of Industrialization

Industrial growth had significant effects on US life. People came to cities to work at the new factories. Industrialization created economic increases worldwide. The large-scale production of goods made them more available to people at a cheaper cost. Industrialization created more jobs, gave people a wider variety of choices, and saved on labor and time.

Disadvantages of industrialization include pollution of air and water, depletion of natural resources, child labor, and the exploitation of the poorer class.

PRACTICE

Pretend you are writing an informative article for a magazine about the effects the railroad, roads, canals, and steamboats had on the United States. You can use pictures to draw how these developments caused changes in the United States, write about it, or do a combination of both.

REVIEW

In this lesson, you learned:

- The development of roads, the railroad, canals, and steamboats impacted the postal service.
- The railroad connecting the East and the West led to factories being built in New England.

Think About It

Without the development of the railroad, what would America look like today?

Draw a line to match the word to its definition.

1. steamboats	**A.** a process that happens in countries when they start to use machines to do work
2. canal	**B.** boats propelled by steam engines
3. industrialization	**C.** a channel of water made by humans for boat transportation or for bringing water to crops

Circle the correct answer.

4. True or False The railroad connected the East and West in the United States.

5. True or False People still settle west using carts pulled by an ox.

6. True or False New England was the spot for factories because they had an abundance of natural resources and farmlands.

7. True or False The Postal Service in the United States is a public service, which keeps mailing costs low.

8. What are the benefits of industrialization? Circle all correct answers.

A. cities grew
B. it helped the environment
C. created economic increases worldwide
D. gave a greater variety of choices

9. What were steamboats used for?

A. to explore the West
B. for a fun river activity
C. to build roads
D. to transport goods and travel

10. How did the railroads affect the Indigenous people? Circle all correct answers.

A. The railroad cut across Indigenous lands.
B. More people settled in the Indigenous lands.
C. Many tribes were relocated from their lands to reservations to make way for the railroad.
D. The railroad affected the Indigenous way of life.

Draw a map of an existing place or a made-up place. Include a key, what the map symbols mean, a canal, and a railroad.

Example of a map key:

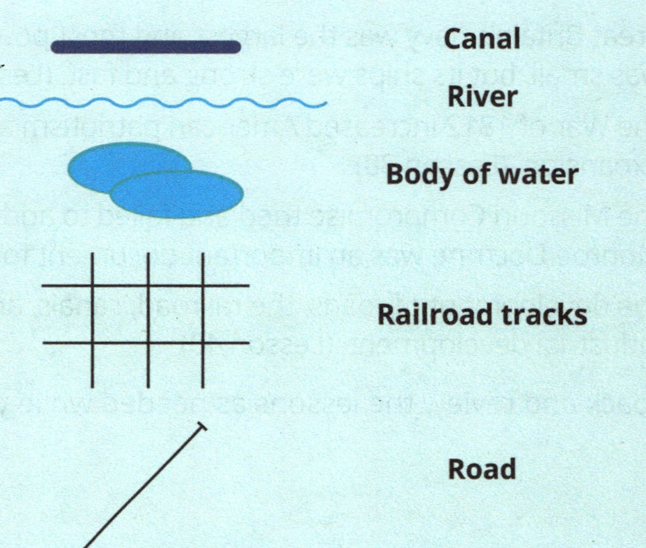

Lesson 41

Chapter 6 Review

By the end of this lesson, you will:

- review the information from the lessons in Chapter 6, "National Growth and Conflict."

Lesson Review

Throughout the chapter, we have learned the following big ideas:

- Great Britain's navy was the largest and most powerful in the world. The US Navy was small, but its ships were strong and fast. (Lesson 37)
- The War of 1812 increased American patriotism and continued westward expansion. (Lesson 38)
- The Missouri Compromise tried and failed to address the issue of slavery. The Monroe Doctrine was an important document for US foreign policy. (Lesson 39)
- The development of roads, the railroad, canals, and steamboats impacted industrial development. (Lesson 40)

Go back and review the lessons as needed while you complete the activities.

Now that you have learned about the War of 1812, let's see if you can win a battle in the War of 1812! Use the information that you have learned about the battles of the War of 1812, and see if you can win the battle.

Search online to find the game Hold the Fort! You will need to get permission to download the web player first.

After playing the game, discuss with your instructor how you fought in the War of 1812. What did you learn about the War of 1812 by playing the game?

The War of 1812

The War of 1812 began June 18, 1812, and lasted until February 16, 1815. Tension had been building for a long time. The United States wanted to expand into areas that belonged to other countries like England.

Neither the United States nor England was ready to fight in a war. England was already at war with France. England needed more sailors, so they captured American sailors and forced them to fight in the British Navy, a process known as impressment. England's Navy had 500 ships, and the United States only had 16.

The war was not an easy win for the United States. The United States was pushed out of Canada by the British. After the Battle of Fort McHenry, Francis Scott Key penned the national anthem, "The Star-Spangled Banner." Another act of patriotism was by First Lady Dolley Madison. While the British burned the US Capitol, she ran into the building and saved documents and a George Washington portrait.

After a few lost battles, there was a turning point in the war. The United States took control of Lake Erie in September 1813, and Tecumseh was killed in the Battle of the Thames. The Americans won the war in February 1815. However, the Battle of New Orleans took place after the treaty was signed. Many people didn't know the war was over. Many Americans died during the War of 1812, and the United States spent time recovering from the war.

The Battle of New Orleans

The Battle of New Orleans took place in January 1815. The war officially ended when the Treaty of Ghent was signed in December 1814. However, the United States was in a set of battles at the time. The final battle of this campaign was in February 1815, about 18 days after the treaty was signed. You may ask, "Why would another battle take place?" At this time, communication was slow. There were also many false news reports about the war ending, so the soldiers may not have believed it. Another reason is that a treaty must be signed to end the war, but it also must be ratified. It wasn't ratified until February 1815.

Describe the turning point in the War of 1812. What happened to the United States during the turning point?

....

....

....

Missouri Compromise, Monroe Doctrine, and Transportation

During the early 1800s, there were many conflicts over slavery. At this time, states were admitted to the Union as either free or slave states. When Missouri and Maine wanted to enter the Union, a conflict arose about whether they should be slave or free states.

The Missouri Compromise of 1820 balanced the slave and free states. Missouri would be a slave state, and Maine would be a free state. Slavery was banned above the 36°30' parallel line and allowed below that line. The compromise failed to deal with the issue of slavery in all states.

Following the War of 1812, the Monroe Doctrine was established. The Monroe Doctrine stated that European nations could not interfere with independent governments in the Western Hemisphere, and the United States would not get involved in existing European colonies.

Transportation improved through canals, steamboats, and roads. The postal system benefited from these modes of transportation. The transcontinental railroad connected the West with the East. Mail was sent more effectively. In addition to the railroad, a national highway called the Cumberland Road connected areas for easier movement.

With an increase in transportation, factories in New England used raw goods to manufacture finished products. New England had many rivers, enabling them to send the finished products to other parts of the country.

The Monroe Doctrine was issued for both the United States and nations in Europe to stop meddling in each other's business. The United States was tired of European nations like Spain, France, and England claiming land in the United States. Europe was tired of the United States interfering in decisions being made in European countries. A doctrine was created and agreed upon so both sides would be content.

How did transportation improve the postal system?

PRACTICE

One Word Doesn't Belong

Circle the word that does not belong in each list. On the line describe why that word does not belong.

1. force   impressment   sailors   territories

2. Dolley Madison   national anthem   patriotism   steamboat

3. free state   manufacturing   Missouri Compromise   slavery

4. capture   colonization   Europe   Monroe Doctrine

5. British Navy   Cumberland Road   Erie Canal   transcontinental railroad

You have probably visited the post office in your town, mailed a letter, or received mail at your home. The postal service is used by millions of people everyday. Did you know that the postal system began as early as 1775? Back then, the postal system relied upon horses to carry the mail from city to city. If a letter was sent to another part of the country, it took months to arrive. When the transcontinental railroad was finished in 1869, the postal system became more efficient. Then a letter only took about a week or two to get to another part of the country. Today, it takes a few days to send a letter from one side of the country to the other side. This is because we can now send letters and packages using aircraft.'

PRACTICE

Cause and Effect

Fill in the cause or effect of each event.

Cause	Effect
England needed sailors and wanted to punish the United States for trading with France.	
	The War of 1812 began due to England's colonization of Lake Erie.
	The United States realized they were not prepared for the war when they lost the first few battles.
British troops set the US Capitol on fire.	
	The Battle of New Orleans took place after the Treaty of Ghent was signed to end the war.

The Monroe Doctrine was written by President James Monroe and heavily influenced by John Quincy Adams. The primary purpose of the Monroe Doctrine was for the United States to expand its area. To do this, they decided to provide something to the European nations in order to stop them from colonizing areas of the United States. Prior to the War of 1812, Great Britain owned the area around Lake Erie, and France owned the Louisiana Territory. Other European nations owned areas in the United States. In return for stopping further colonization in the United States, the United States agreed to stopping their interference in foreign policies.

PRACTICE

Expansion and Transportation Growth

Write a paragraph summarizing how the United States made a plan to allow them to expand and how that led to the growth of transportation.

SHOW WHAT YOU KNOW

Think about what you've learned about in this chapter. Circle how you feel:

4 - I know this chapter really well. I could teach it to someone.

3 - I know this chapter pretty well.

2 - I'm still learning this chapter. I'm not sure about some things.

1 - I am confused. I have a lot of questions about what I've learned.

Talk to your instructor about your answers. When you're ready, ask your instructor for the Show What You Know activity for the chapter.

Chapter 7

American Democracy

Hello! Monty the lion here!

The train crossed a big wide river. I asked Professor Tibbs what this place was. He answered, "We are crossing the Mississippi River."

Maria and I were amazed at its size. I asked, "Who lived here before it was part of the United States?" Professor Tibbs said, "It's another sad story."

Oh no! I was worried, and I'm not lyin'!

Professor Tibbs sighed. "Almost 200 years ago, the Native Americans were taken from their homes. They were forced across this river and had to find new homes."

"Where did they live before?" Maria asked. Professor Tibbs replied, "Native Americans lived all around the United States. Now they can live wherever they want again. But our government once thought they could tell people where to live."

I imagined being forced to leave my home in the savanna. It didn't seem fair. I wanted to give everyone who lost their home a hug.

One of the reasons I wanted to come to America was to learn about democracy. When I rule the savanna in Africa, I want to lead the citizens. What I do not want is to make decisions that hurt people.

But when I traveled across the United States, I learned that the U.S. democracy has a sad history. For democracy to work, citizens and leaders need to care about each other.

I promised I would learn from the mistakes of history. Sometimes learning is hard. When that happens, you know what you do? You roar through it!

What Will I Learn?

This chapter looks at the development of US democracy in the first half of the nineteenth century and the challenges it faced.

Lessons at a Glance

Lesson 42

John Quincy Adams

By the end of this lesson, you will be able to:

- describe what happens when the majority of Electoral College votes are not won by any presidential candidate
- recognize that John Quincy Adams was the sixth president of the United States
- examine the problems some people had with John Quincy Adams's plans for the nation

Academic Vocabulary

Read the following vocabulary words and definitions. Look through the lesson. Can you find each vocabulary word? Underline the vocabulary word in your lesson. Write the page number of where you found each word in the blanks.

- **abolish:** to stop or get rid of something (page ____)
- **abolitionist:** one who works to end the practice of slavery (page ____)
- **constitutional:** anything allowed by or contained in the Constitution (page ____)
- **elect:** to choose a leader from several options, often by voting (page ____)
- **Electoral College:** a body of electors chosen by the voters in each state to elect the president and vice president of the United States (page ____)
- **Federalist Party:** a major political party in the early years of the United States favoring a strong, centralized national government (page ____)
- **tariff:** a tax (page ____)

PLAY

Imagine that you are the leader of a country. Your title is president, and you are in charge of leading the people of your country. What would be important to you? What causes would you fight for? What challenges do you think you would face as president? Do you think it would be an easy job to be president, or would it be a difficult job?

Tell your instructor your plans for your country while you are president.

EXPLORE

Have you ever met someone who had the same job as their mom or dad? Maybe someday you hope to have the same job as one of your parents or another adult close to you. Sometimes people have a family business, which means that the business is run and worked by family members.

Family business does not often refer to politics, but in the case of John Adams and John Quincy Adams, politics was the family business. Both John Adams and his son, John Quincy Adams, were US presidents. John Adams was the second president of the United States of America, and John Quincy Adams was the sixth US president.

Today, you are going to learn more about John Quincy Adams and his plan for the nation.

John Adams

John Quincy Adams

TAKE A CLOSER LOOK

There was one other time a father and son were president of the United States: George H. W. Bush and George W. Bush. George H. W. Bush was the forty-first US president from 1989 to 1993, and his son, George W. Bush, was the forty-third president from 2001 to 2009.

Image, via Wikimedia Commons, is in the public domain.

Image by Eric Draper, via Wikimedia Commons, is in the public domain.

John Quincy Adams

John Quincy Adams was born July 11, 1767, in Braintree, Massachusetts. He was the sixth US president, and he was the first president who was a son of another president. His presidential portrait was the first to be a photograph, not a painting.

He began his political career as a member of the **Federalist Party**, a major political party in the early years of the United States that favored a strong, centralized national government. He later joined the Republican Party. He served in the administrations of all the presidents before him. He was Secretary of State under President James Monroe, the fifth president.

Adams fought against slavery, using his legal skills to help fight for the freedom of African slaves on the slave ship *Amistad*. The legal case began in 1841. The slaves were kidnapped from Africa by Cuban slave owners. The United States had passed a law in 1807 making the importation of enslaved Africans illegal. Adams spoke for four hours and won the case! The court ruled that the Africans were free and could return to their homeland because they were taken illegally from Africa.

He also fought against Congress's "gag rule" that tried to stop members of Congress from talking about **abolishing**, or getting rid of, slavery. Adams argued that the gag rule was not **constitutional**, or legal. After eight years, the gag rule was removed.

John Quincy Adams spoke out against bringing in new slaves from Africa. He was an **abolitionist**, or one who works to end the practice of slavery.

Before 1807, slave hunters captured native Africans from Sierra Leone and sent them to America. Starting in 1807, American laws stopped allowing slaves from other countries to be brought to America. John Quincy Adams's argument for the freedom and return of the Africans to their homeland led to this law.

Why do you think Adams decided to have his presidential portrait photographed instead of being painted like prior presidents?

Plans for the Nation

Adams's views of federal power were more expansive than most of his colleagues. In his first message to Congress in December 1825, he gave a presentation on his ideas for the United States to become an activist national state. He called for legislation sponsoring agriculture, commerce, and manufacturing. His plans included the creation of a national university, an astronomical observatory, and a naval academy.

His ideas came at a time when many Americans felt that governmental authority posed the greatest threat to freedom and liberty. Adams surprised many listeners with the strong statement "liberty is power." He said that the United States was the freest nation on Earth and would become the strongest.

Adams's beliefs and proposals alarmed those who believed in a strict following of the US Constitution's principles. His administration spent more money on internal improvements than the five presidents before him combined! His administration issued a large **tariff**, or tax, on the citizens to pay for these government programs.

John Quincy Adams had many great ideas. He received little support from Congress for his ideas. It was not until the twentieth century that the United States began carrying out the types of national economic and educational improvements Adams suggested.

John Quincy Adams won approval from Congress for several ambitious infrastructure projects. Between 1824 and 1828, the United States Army Corps of Engineers led surveys for several potential roads, canals, railroads, and improvements in river navigation. Adams oversaw major repairs and continued construction on the National Road. Not too long after he left office, the National Road extended from Cumberland, Maryland, to Zanesville, Ohio.

Some people say Adams was ahead of his time. Why do you think people say this?

Electoral College

In other US elections, people **elect** an official solely by popular vote (most voted for person). However, the president and vice president are not elected directly by citizens. Instead, they are selected by "electors" through a process called the **Electoral College**.

Each state gets as many electors as it has members of Congress. There are currently 538 electors. Each state's political parties choose people to serve as potential electors. Each state has their own rules for who they choose and how they are chosen.

After citizens cast their ballots for president, the votes go to a statewide count. In most states, the winner gets all the electoral votes for that state. A presidential candidate needs the votes of at least 270 electors (more than half of all electors) to win the presidential election.

Most of the time, a likely winner is announced on election night after votes are counted. The Electoral College vote takes place in mid-December.

Special Situations

It is possible to win the Electoral College but lose the popular vote. This happened in 2016, in 2000, and three times in the 1800s. If no candidate gets the majority of electoral votes, the House of Representatives chooses the next president. House members cast votes for one of the top three candidates. This has only happened once. In 1824, the House of Representatives elected John Quincy Adams as president.

In this lesson, you learned:

- The electoral process has a system of rules.
- If no candidate gets a majority of the Electoral College votes, the decision goes to Congress.
- Presidential candidates can be very competitive.

Think About It

What would happen if there were somehow a split tie vote in the Electoral College? What would our experience be like if we had two presidents in office at the same time?

Circle the correct answer.

1. The body of electors chosen by the voters in each state to elect the president and vice president of the United States is called the ____________________.

A. federal government

B. election

C. tariff

D. Electoral College

2. The ____________________ Party was a political party founded in the early years of the United States. They believed in a strong, centralized national government.

A. Federalist

B. Nationalist

C. Democrat

D. Greenlane

3. Which person was the sixth president of the United States?

A. Andrew Jackson

B. John Quincy Adams

C. George Washington

D. Abraham Lincoln

4. What happens when the majority of Electoral College votes are not won by any presidential candidate?

A. The previous president stays president.

B. The House of Representatives decides the next president.

C. The United States has a new election.

D. Both people serve as co-presidents.

ONLINE CONNECTION

Look at the map below. This map shows the current Electoral College votes each state has. Using an online search engine, find a map of the Electoral College votes for the presidential election of 1824. How are the two maps alike? How are they different? What do you notice or wonder about these two maps? Discuss your answers with your instructor.

USA MAP VOTING

Democrat
Republican

5. Why did some people disagree with John Quincy Adams regarding his ideas for the country?

....

....

....

....

....

....

Lesson 43

Election of 1828

By the end of this lesson, you will be able to:

- describe the presidential campaigns in 1828 for Andrew Jackson and John Quincy Adams
- identify the method Andrew Jackson wanted to use to fill government jobs

Lesson Review

If you need to review information about John Quincy Adams, please go to the lesson titled "John Quincy Adams."

Academic Vocabulary

Read the following vocabulary words and definitions. Look through the lesson. Can you find each vocabulary word? Underline the vocabulary word in your lesson. Write the page number of where you found each word in the blanks.

- **campaign:** intentional activities, such as public speaking and demonstrating, designed to convince someone to vote for you (page ____)
- **civil service agents:** another term used for government workers (page ____)
- **diplomat:** a person appointed by a national government to conduct official negotiations and maintain political, economic, and social relations with another country or countries (page ____)
- **spoils system:** the phrase used to describe a situation in which a political party gives its voters government jobs for voting in their favor after winning an election (page ____)

A diplomat is a person appointed by a national government to conduct official negotiations and maintain political, economic, and social relations with another country or countries. They help to solve problems and keep the peace.

Between 1794 and 1811, John Quincy Adams served as a US diplomat in several countries. He is known as one of the most successful diplomats.

Pretend you have been chosen to be a diplomat for your country. To what country would you like to be assigned? What problem would you work to solve? Write your answer on the lines below using complete sentences.

....

....

....

EXPLORE

John Quincy Adams was born on July 11, 1767. In 1778, the 10-year-old traveled with his father on his first diplomatic mission to France. He spent most of the next eight years living with his father in Paris, Amsterdam, and London. At 14, Adams was fully fluent in French. This opened up an opportunity for him to be the translator and secretary to St. Petersburg emissary Francis Dana.

Research one of the countries that John Quincy Adams visited. What famous landmarks are there now that were there when Adams visited? Which one would you like to see in person?

Draw a picture of the landmark with a description of what it is. Share your work with your instructor.

TAKE A CLOSER LOOK

John Quincy Adams was a well-traveled and educated person. In 1783, John Quincy Adams returned to Paris as his father's secretary during the treaty negotiations that ended the Revolutionary War.

Presidential Campaigns of 1828

Andrew Jackson, a champion of the common public, was elected president in 1828. This election was significant because of the intense personal attacks. John Quincy Adams, the incumbent, and Andrew Jackson could not have been more different. Adams was the highly educated son of the United States' second president. He traveled to many countries as a **diplomat**. Jackson was an orphan who became a national hero at the Battle of New Orleans.

Adams was known for his foresight and thorough planning. Jackson was known for having fights and brawls. Both men had long careers in public service. They both cared for their fellow citizens but had different views on how to lead the country and what the country really needed.

During their campaigns, both men had wild stories about their pasts printed in newspapers. A **campaign** is intentional activities, such as public speaking and demonstrating, designed to convince someone to vote for you. Each accused the other of bad things.

When the votes were cast, Jackson's accusations against Adams helped him win the election. Adams lost to Jackson, who gained the votes of most of the southern and western states.

TAKE A CLOSER LOOK

During the presidential campaign people talked badly about Rachel, Andrew Jackson's wife. This caused her much stress and sadness. Her health declined, and she died before she could see her husband inaugurated into office.

Why was the presidential campaign and election of 1828 significant? How were the Jackson and Adams campaigns alike and different?

John Quincy Adams Defeated

As president, Adams faced growing anger from Andrew Jackson's supporters in Congress. Some people believe this is why Adams had few accomplishments while in the White House. He envisioned a national program for the country, including federal funding of an interstate roads system, canals, and a national university. However, those who opposed Adams used the Constitution to make the point that those advancements were not allowed.

President Adams's Erie Canal was completed while he was in office. This project linked the Great Lakes to the East Coast and allowed products like grain, whiskey, and farm produce to be transported to the eastern markets.

Adams ran for reelection in 1828. However, Adams's credibility and character were destroyed by unfounded accusations of corruption and criticisms of his unpopular programs. John Quincy Adams lost severely to Andrew Jackson.

To add to his humiliation, at this time in history, Adams was only the second president in US history not to win a second presidential term. The first president to do this was his father in 1800.

After retiring to private life in Massachusetts, Adams ran and won an election to the House of Representatives in 1830. His leadership and work in Congress earned him the nickname "Old Man Eloquent." He lived a long life standing for what he believed in.

Adams's credibility and character were destroyed by accusations that were never confirmed to be true. How would our world be different had Adams won his reelection bid for president? How would history be rewritten?

Why were members of Congress against Adams and his ideas? Why did they agree with Jackson over Adams?

President Jackson's Hiring Practices

Jackson gave federal government positions to his political supporters. This became known as the **spoils system**. The spoils system refers to the phrase "to the victor belongs the spoils." New York Senator William L. Marcy used this term to describe Andrew Jackson's presidential victory in 1828. In general, the spoils system is the phrase used to describe a situation in which a political party gives its voters government jobs for voting in their favor after winning an election.

However, to his opponents, Andrew Jackson's spoils system was the most noticeable way in which he did not keep his promise to fight illegal activities in Washington. Through the spoils system, Jackson replaced many experienced and good government workers, or **civil service agents**, with his own friends and supporters. It was said that many of these new workers had little to no experience for their jobs. These new workers were accused of not being qualified for their jobs and contributing to problems in the government. This stigma about government workers and how the system is run is still common today.

Many saw Jackson's hiring practices as hypocritical. He campaigned on a platform of federal reform to clean out the corruption left behind by John Quincy Adams. But his spoils system saw a slew of appointments based on personal relationships and favors owed, not quality work or eligibility. His hiring practices went against his promise to have a fair and honest government.

In this lesson, you learned:

- John Quincy Adams had passion and dreams for our country.
- John Quincy Adams gave his entire life to serving his fellow humans.
- Andrew Jackson overcame being an orphan to become a US president.

Think About It

Most presidents have served two terms. How would our country be different had John Quincy Adams served two terms instead of only one term?

Please complete each sentence.

1. The ______________________ system is the term used to describe how Andrew Jackson picked government workers.

2. President ______________________ was the president who started the practice of giving government jobs to his political supporters.

Please answer in complete sentences.

3. What did Andrew Jackson do to make government jobs available for his supporters?

4. Describe the presidential campaign of 1828.

Lesson 44

Indian Removal Act

By the end of this lesson, you will be able to:

- summarize the key events in the history of the Cherokee after the Revolutionary War
- identify the main parts of the Indian Removal Act

Lesson Review

If you need to review exploration, please go to the lesson titled "New World."

Academic Vocabulary

Read the following vocabulary words and definitions. Look through the lesson. Can you find each vocabulary word? Underline the vocabulary word in your lesson. Write the page number of where you found each word in the blanks.

- **Cherokee:** the native people of the Southeast Woodlands (page ____)
- **Five Civilized Tribes:** the Native American tribes that adopted white American culture (page ____)
- **Indian Removal Act:** the law that allowed relocation of Native Americans west of the Mississippi River (page ____)
- **Trail of Tears:** the forced march of the Cherokee people from their homeland to the Oklahoma Territory (page ____)

IN THE REAL WRLD

How would you feel if you had to move far away from your homeland? Now imagine that all you could take with you is what you could carry for many miles: about one backpack full.

Make a list of what you would take.

What items would you take with you? What would you miss the most?

....

....

....

In this lesson, you will learn about a situation where this occurred. Thousands and thousands of people were forced to leave their homes and march 2,000 miles (3,218 kilometers). The journey was very harsh and the story is very sad. Let's begin the lesson to find out how and why this happened.

EXPLORE

Imagine life in the forests near the Great Smoky Mountains in the Southeastern United States. This is where a people known as the Cherokee Tribe lived for many generations. The Cherokee lived in these woodland forests and made a life from the natural materials and animals.

The Cherokee hunted deer and turkey that lived in the forest. They used the wood and rocks from the forest to make tools and weapons. They made canoes from timber and used them to fish for trout in the rivers and lakes. The Cherokee lived in villages and grew corn, squash, beans, and other crops.

The Cherokee homeland later became part of the United States, but few Cherokee live on their ancestral homeland today.

Why do you think they are almost all gone? Turn to the next part of the lesson to learn more.

ONLINE CONNECTION

Take a virtual trip to the Museum of the Cherokee Indian in North Carolina. This museum tells the story of the Cherokee way of life and preserves artifacts. You can tour virtual exhibits and view online galleries to learn more about the history, tools, art, and way of life of the Cherokee Nation. If you need help, ask your instructor for assistance navigating the website.

Resurgence Sculpture-Museum of the Cherokee Indian

The Cherokee

The **Cherokee** were the Native Americans of the Southeastern Woodlands. They lived in the present-day states of Georgia, North Carolina, South Carolina, Tennessee, and Alabama. They made simple homes in small villages and lived off of the materials in the forest. They spent time hunting and fishing in the woodlands and growing corn, beans, and squash.

The Cherokee had contact with European settlers as they moved west from the coast. Sometimes they cooperated and traded, while other times there was conflict. After the United States became a country, many Americans urged the Cherokee to become more like the American settlers.

The Cherokee became known as one of the **Five Civilized Tribes**. This name was given to five nations of Native Americans who adopted many customs of the white settlers: the Cherokee, Chickasaw, Choctaw, Creek, and Seminole. The Americans thought of this term as a compliment to the Cherokee. However, it really meant that they thought the Cherokee traditional way of life was inferior.

The Cherokee changed their lifestyle to be more like the Americans who lived nearby. They left the woodlands and moved into cities. Some owned large farms to grow crops using European tools. Some even owned slaves. Many adopted Christianity and learned to speak English. They dressed like the Americans instead of wearing their traditional clothing. Some even married white settlers.

Do you think that the Native Americans should have had to change their way of life to fit in with the settlers nearby? Why or why not?

TAKE A CLOSER LOOK

Sequoyah created an alphabet for the Cherokee in 1825. Before this time, the Cherokee told legends and stories to keep their history. They were known as great storytellers.

Sequoyah's contribution allowed the Cherokee to preserve written records of their history and culture. The Cherokee also created a written Constitution for their nation. Many of the other changes during this time were bad for the Cherokee way of life, but the written language is considered an important innovation.

READ

The Indian Removal Act

Native Americans had a large population in the Southeast. The white Americans desired the land where the Cherokee and other tribes lived. Much of the territory was excellent for growing crops such as cotton, while other parts of the land in North Carolina and Georgia had gold deposits.

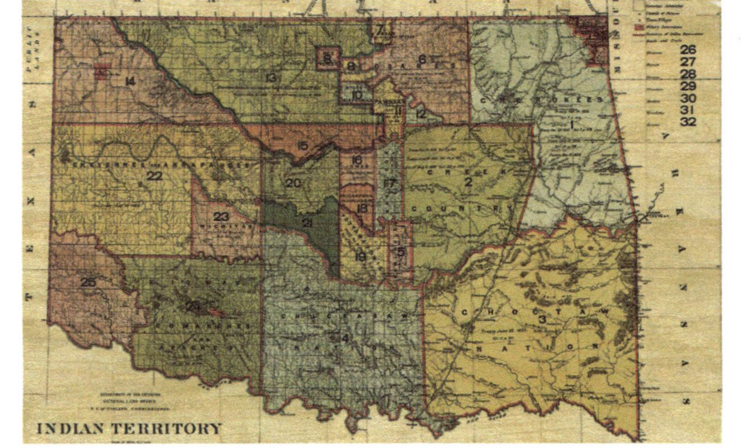

In 1830, the United States passed a law to help the settlers gain the land they wanted. The **Indian Removal Act** stated that native people could be moved off of their land. President Andrew Jackson signed the law. He was known to favor treating native people harshly. The Cherokee and other tribes would be given new land west of the Mississippi River.

Not all Americans agreed with this law. Some white people thought the Cherokee should be able to keep their land. Even the Supreme Court ruled that the Cherokee could keep their lands. Andrew Jackson, however, enforced the law and ignored the courts. The Cherokee were forced to leave.

The Trail of Tears

The Cherokee were forced to move west from their home in the Southeast to the Oklahoma Territory. They were moved by force of the US army. Many Cherokee were taken from their homes, allowed to grab little to no supplies before marching over 2,000 miles (3,218 kilometers). The trip was horrifying. It was endless marching across mountainous lands. Many Cherokee died from heat, cold, disease, or starvation along the way. The path from North Carolina to Oklahoma became known as the **Trail of Tears**. The journey caused unbelievable grief and sorrow.

PRACTICE

Word Bank: Cherokee Civilized Tribes Andrew Jackson gold Indian Removal Act

1. The ______________________ were the largest tribe living in the Southeastern Woodlands.

2. The Five ______________________ adopted the ways of the white settlers nearby.

3. Valuable ______________________ was found on Cherokee lands.

4. The United States passed the ______________________.

5. President ______________________ treated Native Americans harshly.

Effects of the Indian Removal Act

Because of the Indian Removal Act, white settlers gained valuable lands in the Southeastern United States. Some of the lands had the ideal soil and weather for growing cotton. Large cotton plantations sprung up across the region. This made the American South a rich region. However, much of that money was made from the labor of enslaved African Americans.

The Cherokee and other Native Americans were displaced to lands in the west. The journey west was a terrible one. Soldiers forced the Cherokee to leave their homes quickly and begin marching. The weather began as very hot and later became freezing cold. Many Cherokee became ill, and many did not have enough food. Starving and exposed to the elements, thousands of Cherokee died on the long march.

Many Cherokee eventually arrived in the Oklahoma Territory. Those who survived had few possessions and no real way to make a living. Much of the land promised to the Cherokee in Oklahoma was taken from them in later years. Today, many Cherokee still live in Oklahoma, while a few still live on their ancestral lands in North Carolina. They are the largest remaining Native American nation.

Trail of Tears Exhibit at the Cherokee National Museum

In this lesson, you learned:

- The Cherokee lived in the woodlands and spent time hunting, fishing, making art, and telling stories.
- The Five Civilized Tribes adopted many of the ways of white settlers.
- The Indian Removal Act allowed Americans to force the Cherokee off their land and relocate them west of the Mississippi River.
- The march west was done under horrible conditions.
- Many people died along the Trail of Tears.

Think About It

How did life change for the Cherokee during this time period?

Circle the correct answer.

1. True or False   The Cherokee were the native people of the West.

2. True or False   "The Civilized Tribes" adopted the ways of the white settlers.

3. True or False   The Cherokee lands were valuable as sources of gold and cotton production.

4. True or False   President Andrew Jackson supported the removal of native people.

5. True or False   Most Cherokees were allowed to stay in North Carolina.

Answer in complete sentences.

6. What was the Trail of Tears? Describe what happened and how it impacted the Cherokee. Include three pieces of information from the text in your answer.

ONLINE CONNECTION

Who are the native or Indigenous people in your own region? If you live in the United States, they will probably be a Native American tribe. Other locations have other native people, such as First Nations in Canada or the Aboriginal people of Australia. Conduct internet research and find out who the original people of your home region are.

Lesson 45

The Issue of Slavery

By the end of this lesson, you will be able to:

- name Martin Van Buren as the eighth president of the United States
- recognize how the issue of slavery received more attention in the country while Van Buren was president
- describe the main goal of abolitionists

Lesson Review

If you need to review what you have learned about slavery, please go to the lesson titled "Slavery and Trade."

Academic Vocabulary

Read the following vocabulary words and definitions. Look through the lesson. Can you find each vocabulary word? Underline the vocabulary word in your lesson. Write the page number of where you found each word in the blanks.

- **abolitionist:** one who works to end the practice of slavery (page ____)
- **cash crops:** crops that grow well in an area and are worth a lot of money when sold (page ____)
- **Triangle Trade:** a system of trade between Africa, Europe, and the New World (page ____)

The Triangle Slave Trade in the Americas

You have learned that slavery in the United States came from a trading network between Great Britain, the United States, and Africa. Slave traders brought manufactured goods from Europe to Africa, where they took possession of kidnapped people. The enslaved people were brought to America, where they were exchanged for raw goods like sugar or cotton, which were brought back to Europe. Since there were three parts to this system, it is known as the Triangle Trade. The pattern where the United States grew raw materials to ship to Europe continued to grow into the 1830s.

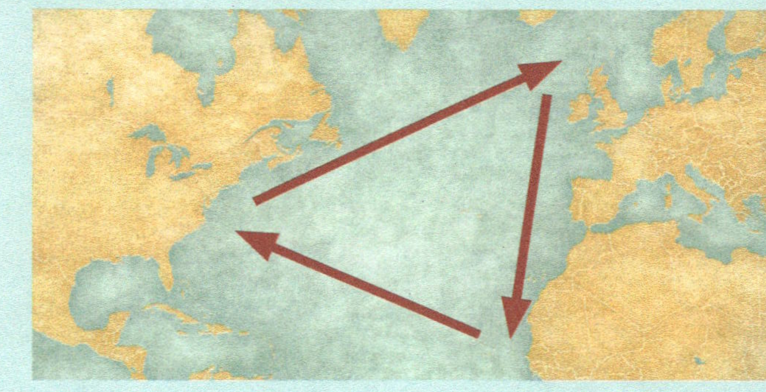

EXPLORE

Should all people have the chance to live a happy and healthy life? What do they need to be fully free and live to their potential?

You have learned that Africans were enslaved by Europeans and brought to the Americas to work. By the 1800s, hundreds of thousands of African Americans lived as enslaved people in the American South. In this lesson, we will learn about how slavery became more of an issue to the American public in the 1830s, and we will learn how some people started to speak out more about the injustice.

Slavery is something that no human being should have to experience. Think about what other basic needs and rights all people should have.

Enslaved African Americans working in a field

Cash Crops

One of the reasons Americans held enslaved people was to become wealthy from free labor. Large plantation farms could grow cash crops such as cotton. Cash crops are crops that grow well in an area and are worth a lot of money when sold. Great Britain and the northern United States valued cotton. These regions had the machines and factories needed to make finished goods, such as clothing, from cotton.

Plantations in the South made fortunes by growing and selling the crop. Because of this, the institution of slavery continued to grow.

Cotton was the most valuable cash crop in the American South.

WRITE

What rights do you think all human beings should have? List at least three ideas.

Presidency of Martin Van Buren

Martin Van Buren was elected as the eighth President of the United States in 1836. Before becoming president, he served as Andrew Jackson's vice president. Jackson was a Southerner from Tennessee, and Van Buren was a Northerner from New York.

At this time, the divide between free states and slave states was the most important issue in the United States. The northern states were industrializing, building factories to manufacture goods. The southern states were based on agriculture. Large plantation farms made southern slaveholders very wealthy but left African Americans living in poverty and misery. More white northerners began to oppose the practice of slavery, while most southern states defended it.

Van Buren was mostly concerned with keeping the United States together even though there was such a deep divide. Therefore, he worked to make compromises that would keep both sides happy. He opposed expansion of slavery into new land but supported keeping the institution. He also allowed southern states to intercept mail from **abolitionists**, one who works to end the practice of slavery, so that their message could not spread to the South.

Van Buren succeeded in his goal to keep the United States together, at least for a little while longer. However, he did not help African Americans gain freedom from slavery. Van Buren's policies delayed the Civil War but did not solve any of America's greatest problems.

TAKE A CLOSER LOOK

The Seminole War

During Martin Van Buren's presidency, the issues of Indian removal and slavery of African Americans intensified as the United States looked toward new land. In the 1700s, members of the Creek Tribe and escaped slaves fled to Florida and formed a new tribe known as the Seminole. Florida was a Spanish colony in the 1700s but had become a US territory in 1821.

Many white American landowners wanted the Seminole moved from Florida to the West because they felt the tribe encouraged enslaved people to flee. The US Army attacked the Seminole in 1836 and removed most of the tribe to the Oklahoma Territory.

Tuko-See-Mathla by Charles Bird King is in the public domain.

READ

La Amistad

In 1839, national attention was drawn to a single ship, *La Amistad*. The *Amistad* was a Spanish slave ship transporting kidnapped Africans to Cuba. During the trip, the enslaved Africans revolted. They killed the captain and took over control of the *Amistad*. The Africans ordered the *Amistad* crew to sail the boat back to Africa. However, the *Amistad* was intercepted in American waters near New York and Connecticut.

The Spanish wanted the Africans to be put on trial for mutiny and for killing the captain. The courts considered the case and ruled in favor of the Africans. The court treated the Africans as men and not as property. They were justified in the revolt as self-defense because they had been kidnapped. The *Amistad* became a symbol of the abolition movement. Different opinions about the case further brought the issue of slavery to attention throughout the United States.

La_Amistad_(ship).jpg by unknown is in the public domain.

The Liberator

William Lloyd Garrison was an abolitionist from Boston. Garrison was opposed to slavery and wanted to spread the message. He founded a newspaper called *The Liberator.* Many white people who were against slavery and many free African Americans read the newspaper. As Garrison gained more followers, he helped found the American Anti-Slavery Society. The members of the organization worked to alert the public to the injustice and horror of slavery. Garrison encouraged abolitionists to work to end slavery completely instead of compromising with slave states.

WRITE

The abolitionists used the story of *La Amistad* as a symbol of their cause. They celebrated the bravery of the Africans and the just result of the court case. Do you think the court was right to side with the African men? Explain why.

READ

Texas

During Van Buren's presidency, the fate of Texas became a large issue. Texas won its independence from Mexico in 1836. Although Texas would not join the United States until 1845, talk about annexation began almost immediately. Many Texas leaders had southern roots. Sam Houston was the first president of the Republic of Texas. Before moving to Texas, he served as governor of Tennessee.

Abolitionists opposed the annexation of Texas because Texans wanted to be a slave state. President Van Buren agreed with the abolitionists, but he angered many voters in the South. Because of the Texas issue, the Seminole War, and his inability to make enough people happy through compromise, Martin Van Buren was voted out of office in 1840 after serving one term. Van Buren's replacement, William Henry Harrison, died after 18 days in office. Harrison was replaced by Vice President John Tyler. These events led to the Civil War, which you will learn about in later lessons.

REVIEW

In this lesson, you learned:

- Martin Van Buren was the eighth president of the United States.
- Van Buren tried to keep the United States together by making compromises between slave and free states.
- More Americans became abolitionists and worked to end slavery.

Think About It

Why do you think that Martin Van Buren made compromises instead of working to end slavery?

PRACTICE

Choose the word that best completes each sentence below:

Word Bank: Texas Martin Van Buren abolitionist *The Liberator* *La Amistad* Seminole

1. Kidnapped Africans revolted on board ______________________.
2. ______________________ fought to end slavery across the United States.
3. ______________________ tried to make compromises between free and slave states.
4. The territory of ______________________ wanted to join the United States.
5. Anti-slavery activists published a newspaper called ______________________.

Circle the correct answer.

1. True or False Martin Van Buren was elected president of the United States.

2. True or False Most abolitionists lived in the South.

3. True or False Slavery was growing larger because cotton was a valuable cash crop.

4. True or False Some African Americans who escaped slavery joined the Seminole Tribe and fought against the US Army.

5. True or False Martin Van Buren tried to end slavery.

6. Slavery received national attention during the 1830s. List three events that brought more attention to the issue.

ONLINE CONNECTION

Many abolitionists were African American slaves or former slaves who fought against slavery. Using an online search engine, research some of the Black abolitionists who had an important role in helping to free slaves or fight for the end of slavery.

Frederick Douglass was an important Black abolitionist.

Lesson 46

Chapter 7 Review

By the end of this lesson, you will:

- review the information from the lessons in Chapter 7, "American Democracy."

Lesson Review

Throughout the chapter, we have learned the following big ideas:

- If no candidate gets a majority of the Electoral College votes, the decision goes to Congress. (Lesson 42)
- Andrew Jackson and John Quincy Adams ran very competitive campaigns during the 1828 election. (Lesson 43)
- The Indian Removal Act allowed Americans to force the Cherokee off their land and relocate them west of the Mississippi River. (Lesson 44)
- The issue of slavery received more attention in the country while President Van Buren was in office. Abolitionists were people who worked to end slavery. (Lesson 45)

Go back and review the lessons as needed while you complete the activities.

Research elections from colonial America and elections today online. What is the importance of the Electoral College? What do you think has changed in the Electoral College from when it started to the present time?

John Quincy Adams

John Quincy Adams was born on July 11, 1767. He was the sixth President of the United States and the first president who was a son of a president. During his political career, he was a Federalist. He served in the administrations of all the presidents that came before him. John Quincy Adams had a lot of great ideas. However, he received very little support from Congress. The United States did not start to carry out the types of national economic and educational improvements suggested by Adams until the twentieth century.

John Quincy Adams

The Election of 1828

The Electoral College met on December 3. Adams won almost exactly the same states that his father won in the election of 1800: the New England states, New Jersey, and Delaware. In addition, Adams picked up Maryland. Andrew Jackson won everything else, which resulted in a landslide victory for him. Jackson defeated Adams by an electoral vote of 178 to 83 after a campaign in which personalities and slander played a larger part than ever before. The election of 1828 was unique in that nominations were no longer made by Congressional caucuses but by conventions and the state legislatures. John Quincy Adams was re-nominated by the National Republicans. His running mate was Secretary of the Treasury Richard Rush.

Victory for Andrew Jackson

The election of 1828 shocked many people. Adams swept New England but won only three states outside of his home region. Jackson became the first president whose home state was neither Massachusetts nor Virginia. The election began the Jacksonian Democracy, marking the transition from the First Party System to the Second Party System.

Indian Removal Bill

The Indian Removal Act was signed into law on May 28, 1830, by US President Andrew Jackson. The Act was enforced under Andrew Jackson's administration and that of Martin Van Buren, which extended until 1841. The Act was strongly supported by southerners.

The Indian Removal Act stated that all Native Americans living east of the Mississippi River were required to move west of the Mississippi River. The Act was passed because Americans wanted to settle on Native American land. It was considered controversial because the Supreme Court ruled in favor of the tribes' cause wherein the state of Georgia (which was actively seeking to evict the Indian inhabitants) was told it had no right to force their removal. Nevertheless, the president ordered their removal.

Slavery

The history and growth of slavery in colonial America was tied to the rise of land cultivation, particularly the boom in the production of tobacco (in Virginia and Maryland) and rice (in the Carolinas). The Royal African Company's expansion in 1672 resulted in a growing surge of the transport of Africans to the colonies.

Slavery formed a cornerstone of the British Empire in the 18th century. Every colony had slaves, from the southern rice plantations in Charles Town, South Carolina, to the northern wharves of Boston. Slavery was more than a labor system. It also influenced every aspect of colonial thought and culture.

Did you know that the first enslaved Africans arrived in Virginia in 1619, and that the practice of slavery would continue uninterrupted for the next 246 years in North America? What we must remember is that British interests dictated many things, and slavery was only one component. England's economic expansion in the sixteenth century owed largely to her navy, whose vast outreach across the world's oceans allowed the British government to create new modes of commerce and wealth.

PRACTICE

Vocabulary Activity

Fill in the blank with an answer from the Word Bank.

Word Bank: Five Civilized Tribes abolitionist Indian Removal Act past Trail of Tears Transatlantic Slave Trade

1. The ______________________ is the European practice that started in the late 1400s to ship arms, textiles, and other goods to Africa and crops like sugar, tobacco, cotton, and coffee to Europe. It also enslaved people in the Americas.
2. An ______________________ is one who works to end the practice of slavery.
3. The ______________________ are Native American tribes that adopted white American culture.
4. Any time that has already happened is called the ______________________.
5. The ______________________ was the forced march of the Cherokee people from their homeland to the Oklahoma Territory.
6. A law that allowed relocation of Native Americans west of the Mississippi River was called the ______________________.

Before completing the fill in the blanks, review the words in the word bank in your mind. Discuss with your instructor any words that are difficult. Many of these vocabulary words refer to an actual situation that arose during this time period. Do you remember the Trail of Tears after the Indian Removal Act? The Transatlantic Slave Trade caused many problems in the South. What role did the abolitionists have during this time?

PRACTICE

Pros and Cons of the Electoral College

The Electoral College is a process, not a place. The Founding Fathers established it in the Constitution, in part, as a compromise between the election of the president by a vote in Congress and election of the president by a popular vote of qualified citizens. Pretend you are a voter during the election of 1828. Present an argument, either pro or con, on the Electoral College. It may be helpful to organize the pros and cons in a t-chart and then pick one to write your argument.

PROS	CONS

Electoral College

We still use the Electoral College today. The Electoral College is the formal body which elects the President and Vice President of the United States. Each state has as many electors in the Electoral College as it has representatives and senators in the United States Congress.

PRACTICE

Venn Diagram

On May 28, 1830, Congress passed the Indian Removal Act, beginning the forced relocation of thousands of Native Americans in what became known as the Trail of Tears. Using a Venn diagram, compare both sides of the argument: Native Americans vs. Congress. In the center of the Venn diagram, put the land being fought over by both groups.

NATIVE AMERICANS

BOTH

CONGRESS

Think about what you've learned about in this chapter. Circle how you feel:

4 - I know this chapter really well. I could teach it to someone.

3 - I know this chapter pretty well.

2 - I am still learning this chapter. I am not sure about some things.

1 - I am confused. I have a lot of questions about what I've learned.

Talk to your instructor about your answers. When you're ready, ask your instructor for the Show What You Know activity for the chapter.

Chapter 8

Growth in the East

Hi there! Once again, Monty the lion is at your service.

Maria, Professor Tibbs, and I were heading out West. Along the way, we learned so much about the people and history of the United States.

Every day I learn something else that will help me be a better king.

But there is so much to do before I go home. So let's roar through this together!

The Mississippi River was far behind us. We were speeding out West quickly.

I asked Professor Tibbs when the railway was built. He explained that the first railway built across the United States was completed in 1869. I asked, "So did anyone go west before that?"

It turns out that people would take wagons across the country. Other people would take boats on the Mississippi River. But getting from the East to the West was very hard.

Professor Tibbs explained, "The country could not be that big. There was no way to communicate from Pennsylvania to California."

I didn't exactly know what he meant. But Maria did! She said, "Technology makes the world smaller. With railways, you can get from east to west. With telephones, people can talk to each other from far away."

Professor Tibbs said, "You have a very smart wife!" I know I do! I am so happy I get to see this beautiful country with Maria and Professor Tibbs.

What Will I Learn?

This chapter looks at the economic and technological advancements on the eastern seaboard during the nineteenth century.

Lessons at a Glance

Lesson 47

Railroads and Canals

By the end of this lesson, you will be able to:

- describe how canals were essential in beginning to connect the eastern and western United States
- evaluate supply and demand, using steamboat companies as an example
- analyze the role railroads played in connecting cities and helping them grow

Academic Vocabulary

Read the following vocabulary words and definitions. Look through the lesson. Can you find each vocabulary word? Underline the vocabulary word in your lesson. Write the page number of where you found each word in the blanks.

- **canal:** a channel of water made by humans for boat transportation or for bringing water to crops (page ____)
- **demand:** the number of people wanting to buy what is for sale (page ____)
- **irrigation:** brings water into your home from a local water supply (page ____)
- **railroad:** a track or set of tracks made of steel rails along which passenger and freight trains run (page ____)
- **supply:** the amount of a product that someone has for sale (page ____)

PLAY

Pretend you are running a local railroad station. Where does this railroad go? How many stops does it make? What features of this railroad station make it memorable? Create your railroad station and invite your instructor to purchase tickets for one of your destinations.

EXPLRE

Have you ever wanted to go on a vacation on a big boat or ocean liner? They didn't always look that way. The first boats that traveled from place to place were called steamboats and were used to bring products from one place to another. Now, we have ports for cruise ships and ocean liners all over the world. Which port would you like to visit?

Cruise ships accommodate thousands of passengers

ONLINE CONNECTION

Before you start learning about canals and their importance in connecting the Eastern and Western United States, search online for videos and pictures of famous canals, such as the Erie Canal, the Panama Canal, and the Suez Canal.

Port in the Mediterranean Sea

Harbor in Greece

READ

Canals in the 1800s

Waterways and railroads linked the east and west regions of the United States. Produce moved on small boats from farms to ports. Large steamships carried goods and people. Railroads connected towns, providing faster transport.

A **canal** is a channel of water made by humans for boat transportation or for bringing water to crops. Canals are used for irrigation, travel, and shipping. **Irrigation** brings water into homes from a local water supply. It is used by more than half the farmers in the world to water their crops. Canals are dug in the ground and lined with rocks or steel to make them stronger, which also keeps water from leaking.

Canals created a transportation revolution in the early nineteenth century. Using canal locks, ships can sail up or downhill. Regional canals developed into a national network of waterways. For example, the Erie Canal connects Lake Erie to the Hudson River, which feeds into the Atlantic Ocean. Nearly every major city in New York is along the Erie Canal. It links Buffalo, Rochester, Syracuse, Utica, and Albany with New York City.

Erie Canal, New York

TAKE A CLOSER LOOK

The Erie Canal and Slavery

One unintended result of the Erie Canal was to create a stronger divide between the North and the South about slavery. People from the North and South could now visit other areas of the country more easily, giving northerners stronger opinions about how wrong slavery was. Abolitionists, like Frederick Douglass, Sojourner Truth, and Harriet Tubman, were able to travel more easily using the Erie Canal too. They used the Erie Canal to connect with each other and to spread their message of abolition. The North also became less dependent on the South for trade.

READ

Railroads Connected Cities

A **railroad** is a track or set of tracks made of steel rails along which passenger and freight trains run. The railroad industry played an important role in building cities between 1877 and 1920. People resettled to cities where factory demand for labor meant employment, and to western cities developing along railways. Railroads facilitated the transportation of equipment and steel for construction.

Companies employed Irish and Chinese workers in the 19th century. Once the rails were laid, companies needed a large workforce to keep the trains running. By 1880, 400,000 men—nearly 2.5 percent of the nation's workforce—worked in the railroad industry. The work was dangerous and low-paying, and companies relied on immigrant labor.

TAKE A CLOSER LOOK

The Great Railroad Strike of 1894

The railroad opened the way for settlement of the American West, provided new economic opportunities, stimulated development of communities, and tied the country together. The railroads were shut down during the Great Railroad Strike of 1894. While the railroads were shut down, the true importance of the railroads was fully realized. Can you imagine life without railroads? How would people get to work in cities? How would we travel or distribute goods across the country?

Steamboats, Supply, and Demand

Supply and demand is the relationship between sellers and buyers. **Supply** is the amount of a product someone has for sale. **Demand** is the number of people wanting to buy what is for sale. When you shop for new clothes or a video game, you tell stores what types of items and services you are willing to purchase. Companies use information about what you buy when they decide what to offer in stores. In a successful economy, businesses sell what buyers want, and shoppers spend their money.

Before steamboats, people traveled rivers using keelboats, which are big, flat-bottomed boats. River currents allowed them to travel easily downstream. To travel upstream, keelboats had crew members with long poles or teams of oxen on shore to pull the boat along. It took six weeks to travel down the Mississippi River, but the return trip took four or five months.

This changed when steam power enabled boats to travel. Each boat used a large boiler heated by a furnace to travel five to eight miles per hour. In the United States, John Fitch built the first steamboat, which successfully began to travel on the Delaware River on August 22, 1787. Steamboats contributed greatly to the economy of the eastern United States. They transported agricultural and industrial supplies. Between 1814 and 1834, steamboat arrivals in New Orleans increased from 20 to 1,200 each year. These boats transported passengers, cotton, sugar, and other goods.

In this lesson, you learned:

- Canals were important in connecting the east and west.
- Railroads connected the Eastern and Western United States, allowing for trade and travel.
- Supply and demand is the relationship between sellers and buyers.
- Steamboats allowed people to transport goods more easily upstream.

Think About It

What do you think it would be like if there were no railroads? How would businesses succeed if they didn't know what people wanted?

Match the word to definition.

1. ____ canal
2. ____ irrigation
3. ____ supply
4. ____ demand
5. ____ railroad

A. a track or set of tracks made of steel rails

B. the amount of a product that someone has for sale

C. the number of people wanting to buy what is for sale

D. a channel of water made by humans for boat transportation or for bringing water to crops

E. something that brings water into homes from a local water supply

Read each sentence. Circle True or False.

6. True or False Irrigation is only important to farmers.

7. True or False Canals were built to connect waterways from the east to west coasts.

Complete the sentences in this short paragraph.

8. A ____________ is a track or set of tracks made of steel rails along which passenger and freight trains run. The railroad industry played an important role in building ____________ across the country. People could resettle to cities where ____________ demand for labor meant employment. The building of railroads opened the way for the ____________ of the West.

People have always enjoyed being on a railroad. When railroads first came into existence, they created many jobs. Listen to the song "I've Been Working on the Railroad." Discuss what the lyrics in the song mean with your instructor.

Lesson 48

Cities and Farm Life

By the end of this lesson, you will be able to:

- identify the positive and negative outcomes of living in a city
- explain the connection between agriculture and the South and identify the reasons crops grew well there
- describe the characteristics of a plantation
- describe the differences between living on a small farm and a plantation
- explain how jobs located in cities and ports, such as blacksmithing, were important to farms

Academic Vocabulary

Read the following vocabulary words and definitions. Look through the lesson. Can you find each vocabulary word? Underline the vocabulary word in your lesson. Write the page number of where you found each word in the blanks.

- **agriculture:** farming (page ____)
- **plantation:** a large farm (page ____)

Do you ever wonder what schools were like long ago? How do you think they were different? Search online to see schools then and schools now. Talk to your instructor about your findings.

One-Room Schoolhouse

EXPLORE

Do you ever wonder what it was like to live in the 1800s? Do you think about jobs that people had and what their houses looked like? With your instructor's help, find pictures and articles online showing jobs from the 1800s and what they were like. Do we still do any of these jobs today?

What do you think a blacksmith does?

What do you think a cooper does?

What does a shoemaker do?

What does a barber do?

CREATE

After researching online the jobs that people had during this time, pick four that you would like to focus on. Get a piece of white drawing paper and divide it into fourths. Label each square with the name of a job, cut out pictures you found, glue them in the square, and write a sentence describing what the job is.

For example, you may pick a carpenter and put some pictures of a carpenter making furniture. Then, you can add a sentence stating, "A carpenter learns his trade from an accomplished carpenter and practices making objects from wood before becoming a carpenter."

READ

Living in a City

The growth of trade, manufacturing, and transportation brought many changes to cities in the North. Cities took on an important role in determining the culture in the North. Merchants, manufacturers, wage earners, and new business owners brought new ideas to city life. Villages outside the city became strong centers of community activities. Both religious and educational institutes were organized. Most cities had schools and churches. Public education grew rapidly, although only boys went to secondary school and college was reserved mostly for the wealthy.

The soil in the northern United States was better for smaller farmlands rather than the larger farmlands in the South. Many large cities were established in the northern United States, such as New York City and Philadelphia.

After the 1830s, harbors and streets improved, sanitation systems were developed, and police forces were created. The cities continued to grow with more job opportunities and new industries beginning to form.

Transportation improved as the size of the United States more than doubled. By 1860 there were over 88,000 miles of surfaced roads. Canals, mostly built in the North, were the cheapest source of transportation.

Erie Canal, New York

New York City, New York

READ

Agriculture in the South

The warm climate and fertile soil of the South made it ideal for **agriculture**, or farming. Many farms grew crops like cotton, rice, and tobacco. Because agriculture was so profitable for southerners, few saw a need for industrial development. Most of the labor force worked on farms. There were no large cities, except for New Orleans, Louisville, Charleston, and Richmond. Most cities were located on rivers and coasts and used as ports to send agricultural produce to Europe.

Life on a Plantation

The plantation system developed in the South as British colonists arrived in Virginia and divided the land into large areas suitable for farming. A piece of this land was called a **plantation**, or a large farm which specialized in farming one type of crop. The plantation system dominated the culture of the South.

The term *plantation* arose as southern settlements and colonial expansion revolved around agriculture. Tobacco and cotton crops were very profitable. Wealthy landowners got wealthier, and the use of slave labor increased.

Life in the fields meant working very long days with very little food to eat. Slave workers often lived in shacks on the outskirts of the main plantation.

PLAY

With the help of your instructor, find an article online written by someone who worked on a plantation. Pretend you are this person. Write a diary entry using a date from that time period or act out what you think this person might have done during a day in their life.

WRITE

Why was the South ideal for agriculture? Describe life on a plantation. What is a plantation, and what was it used for? What kind of people worked there, and what were they growing?

....

....

....

....

....

City and Port Jobs

Ports are an important part of the economy in coastal regions. The ports supplied jobs. Shippers and merchants worked at the ports, loading and unloading ships filled with goods.

New York City was one of the most important port cities in the Middle Colonies. The Hudson River made trade easier. Farmers, fur traders, and lumber workers could float their goods down the river to New York City.

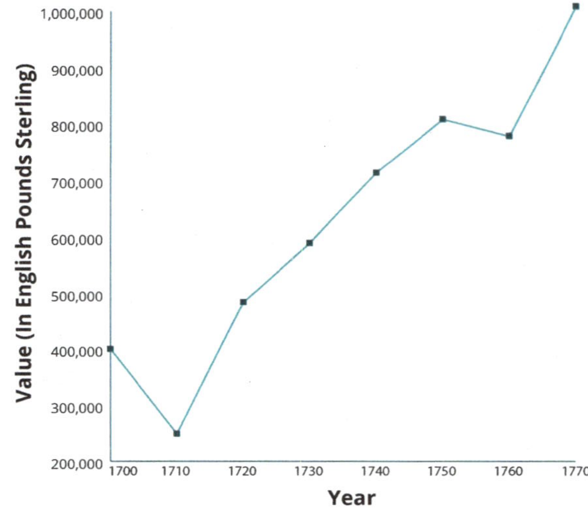

Port workers made it possible for growth in exports to European countries from the United States.

Many other jobs in cities helped farmers export products and make money. The jobs also used raw materials to make products. Blacksmiths used iron to create horseshoes and farming tools. Coopers made barrels out of wood. Carpenters and shipbuilders used wood to build houses and ships. Masons and bricklayers worked with stone and clay to pave streets and construct buildings. Dressmakers and tailors used wool, linen, and cotton to make clothing.

In this lesson, you learned:

- Cities played an important role in determining the culture of the North.
- The warm climate and fertile soil of the South made it ideal for large farms, or plantations.
- Plantations caused an increase in the use of slave labor.
- Cities and ports helped farmers and plantation owners export their goods.
- Blacksmithing and shipbuilding were two important jobs in cities and ports.

Think About It

How do you think life was different in a city and a small farm?

Name a job held by someone working at a port. Name a job held by someone working in a city that helped farmers.

Read each sentence. Circle True or False.

1. True or False Cities took on an important role in determining the culture in the North.

2. True or False Canals, mostly built in the South, were the cheapest source of transportation.

3. True or False After the 1830s, harbors and streets improved and sanitation systems were created.

4. True or False Tobacco and cotton crops were exceptionally profitable on plantations.

5. True or False Ports were not an important part of the economy in coastal regions.

Answer the following question in complete sentences.

6. Compare life in the North with life in the South. Be sure to include what is the same and what is different.

....

....

....

....

....

....

....

....

....

Using materials available (cardboard, molding clay, toys) create one of the following:

- a port that resembles one in the 1800s
- an old schoolhouse
- a plantation

Lesson 49

Technological Advances

By the end of this lesson, you will be able to:

- analyze the reasons manufacturing mostly occurred in the Northeast
- identify advancements in technology that helped improve work on farms and in cities
- describe why inventors would need patents to protect the inventions they make
- evaluate the costs and benefits of technology

Lesson Review

If you need to review the difference between city and farm living, please go to the lesson titled "City and Farm Life."

Academic Vocabulary

Read the following vocabulary words and definitions. Look through the lesson. Can you find each vocabulary word? Underline the vocabulary word in your lesson. Write the page number of where you found each word in the blanks.

- **combine:** a farming vehicle that harvests crops (page ____)
- **factory:** a building where products are made or put together with machines (page ____)
- **Industrial Revolution:** a time period when many new inventions led to changes in how products were made (page ____)
- **loom:** a machine that weaves thread into cloth or fabric (page ____)
- **textile:** woven cloth and fabric (page ____)

Chicago

Chicago, Illinois was a small, swampy settlement in the 1700s. By 1880, it was the largest city outside the East Coast. Chicago was a center of the Industrial Revolution—or time period when many new inventions led to changes in how products were made. At this time, new inventions changed life for many Americans.

The railroad and canals connected the city to all areas of the country. Factories and processing plants turned crops from farmers' fields into canned products to send to stores. Workers used machines to make products faster than ever before.

EXPLORE

Back in the 1800s, you may have worked in a factory. A **factory** is a large building where products are made or put together with machines. Many boys and girls around your age worked in factories in the 1800s. Children aged 7 to 13 often worked long hours and operated dangerous machinery. They did not have a chance to go to school.

It must have been scary to work in a factory as a child at this time. There were not many laws to protect workers. There were no safety standards, and facilities were usually in a terrible, unclean condition. Smoke from the factory was heavy, and it was hard to breathe.

PLAY

Compare the lives of children in the 1800s and today by acting out a typical day in the life of two children.

- For one of the characters, show the life of a regular child your age today. You may want to show someone eating breakfast, going to school, or playing sports.
- Then have someone act out the life of a child your age working in a factory in the 1800s. Make sure to note how the child works long hours and operates dangerous machines.

Use action figures, dolls, or stuffed animals as the characters. Perform the routine for your instructor or family members. Ask the audience to compare the situation of the two characters.

WRITE

Would you have liked to work in a factory every day? Why or why not?

READ

Northern Industry

Before the **Industrial Revolution**, most Americans lived on farms. They made things by hand for their own use. Everything changed as new technology changed the way people lived and worked. Since the southern United States had profitable farming land, much of the industry ended up in the Northeast.

The first large industry was textile mills in Massachusetts. **Textiles** are woven cloth and fabric. Mills were factories where a large water wheel provided power to many machines. Later, steam power drove the gears even faster.

The mills took the raw material of cotton from the South and sewed it into clothing, blankets, and other cloth materials. Most of the workers in these mills were young girls and women from nearby farms. They operated powered **looms**, or large machines that spun cotton fibers into cloth. One effect of the mill was to allow women to enter the workforce in large numbers for the first time.

Following this model, factories began to build all types of products at a faster rate. Engineers discovered ways to burn coal to drive steam engines. These new engines made machines work faster. There were many benefits as people had more products to use than they had ever dreamed.

However, life in the new urban city had drawbacks. There was lots of dirt and soot from smoke. People were packed together in inadequate housing. There were not enough services or facilities for everyone, and garbage was thrown out in the streets. Disease outbreaks were common.

IN THE REAL WORLD

Interchangeable Parts

For most of history, skilled workers made tools and goods by hand. These items were of good quality, but the system was inefficient. If an item broke or stopped working, a new one would be made from scratch.

Soon, factory owners used interchangeable parts. Instead of making one part, they made hundreds at a time. The parts would be made into a mold and reproduced. If anything broke, a new part could be inserted. Products could be made faster.

READ

Advances in Farming Technology

The advances of industry were also used by farmers across the country. Farmers used to rely on the physical labor of people and animals. However, new inventions changed everything.

A blacksmith named John Deere made one of the first important inventions. His steel plow was much lighter and prepared fields better than old iron plows. Eventually, the John Deere company and others began making tractors.

Other farming inventions included the thresher and the combine. The thresher machine beat wheat plants so the edible part came out. Later, the combine was invented. The **combine** is a large vehicle that harvests crops. Much of the work previously done by hand was done by machines.

This was the start of a big change in how people lived. Fewer people were needed to operate a farm and grow food. Many people moved to cities to find other types of work.

The Cotton Gin

Eli Whitney invented a mechanical device to separate seeds from cotton. The cotton engine was nicknamed the *cotton gin.* It used a motor, wire hooks, and a screen to clean the seeds out of the cotton quickly. Previously, they had to be picked out by hand. The tough job of picking and cleaning cotton was often done by enslaved people on southern plantations.

thresher machine

combine

cotton gin

The Patent Office

Where did all these new technologies come from? They were designed by talented inventors.

The inventors wanted protection from others copying their ideas. The federal government developed a type of document called a *patent*. Patents are written descriptions and drawings of a new invention. If the idea is new, the inventor will be granted a patent. This gives the patent holder the right to produce and sell the new invention. If a company wants to make and sell the product, they must negotiate with the patent holder. Usually, the company pays a small percentage of each sale to the patent holder. The company and the inventor each make some profit, and the buyers are helped as well.

In this lesson, you learned:

- During the Industrial Revolution, people began to work in large factories in the Northeast.
- Technological inventions made workers more productive.
- New machines such as tractors made farming easier.
- Inventors protected their ideas with patents.

Think About It

What advancements are making life easier today? Are there any drawbacks to the new technology?

Since machines could do the work for people, what do you think all of the farm workers did after these inventions became common?

Use the words from the Word Bank to complete each sentence.

Word Bank:	combine	factory	loom	Northeast	Industrial Revolution
	textile	southern	patent	Revolutionary War	

1. The ______________________ was the time period when new inventions changed life for many Americans.
2. The ______________________ was a machine used to spin cotton threads into clothing.
3. A ______________________ was issued to protect an invention.
4. The ______________________ was a vehicle that harvested crops.
5. A ______________________ is a large building used to make or assemble products.
6. The ______________________ United States had profitable farming land, so much of the industry ended up in the ______________________.

Answer the following question in complete sentences.

7. The change to a more industrial society helped people get more products. However, there were also many negative consequences. Explain two negative outcomes of the advancements in technology.

Circle True or False.

8. True or False The Industrial Revolution changed the way many people lived.

9. True or False Farmers did not use any new inventions.

10. True or False Many children worked in factories.

11. True or False New factories caused pollution.

12. True or False Inventors protected their ideas with patents.

Research the Lowell mills in Massachusetts. Discover facts about how the mill was founded, how it operated, and what products were made. Then learn about the Lowell mill girls. These young ladies proved that women could join the workforce and advocated for workers' rights. Discuss your findings with your instructor.

Lesson 50

Communication

By the end of this lesson, you will be able to:

- describe how the United States Postal Service developed
- describe how a telegraph works
- identify examples of businesses that used the telegraph

Lesson Review

If you need to review how technology improved during the 1800s, please go to the lesson titled "Technological Advances."

Academic Vocabulary

Read the following vocabulary word and definition. Look through the lesson. Can you find the vocabulary word? Underline the vocabulary word in your lesson. Write the page number of where you found the word in the blank.

- **telegraph:** a system that sends messages across an electric wire (page ____)

The Pony Express

You probably have seen the mail carrier bring letters to your mailbox. The federal postal system didn't always exist as we know it—especially in the West. Private companies such as the Pony Express and Wells Fargo carried mail for a fee.

The Pony Express was a route from Missouri to California. The riders had to be young and small, so they weighed the least amount possible. They carried bags of letters across mountains and plains with few supplies. The Pony Express was eventually replaced by faster communication systems.

EXPLORE

People today often take communication for granted. We live in a world where you can make a phone call or send a text message to talk to others instantly. They can be close by or thousands of miles away.

If we traveled back in time a few hundred years, we would see nothing like this. Most people lived their entire life in their small town or village. They had no way to get messages out to anyone who lived far away. They may try writing a letter and asking someone who was traveling to deliver it. But of course, that was only if the traveler could even find the recipient.

Only the most important news would ever get to you, and that would only come in a newspaper that was weeks behind the events. You would probably not even know what it was like outside your own immediate area. Going to another state or country was a rare event. People were very isolated compared to how we experience life today.

What inventions made communication faster in the 1800s? What were some of the steps between the old way and our modern high technology?

PLAY

Use action figures, stuffed animals, and household objects to play Pony Express. You will act out the way delivering mail was a difficult challenge in the past. Make barriers like mountains and rivers. Place dangerous animals along the path. Have an animal travel along the path to deliver the mail.

READ

The US Postal Service

The idea for a postal service goes back to one of the best known Americans—Benjamin Franklin. During colonial times, the delivery of mail was not very effective. Big wagons full of mail would arrive in one of the big towns such as Philadelphia or Boston every few months. Sometimes letters were sent by boat back to England. You were lucky if your letter even was delivered. The 13 colonies needed a much better system.

Franklin became the official postmaster. He inspected the way that mail worked and made many improvements. He established regular schedules and expanded the number of places mail carriers would go. Rules were set for how often mail was delivered and how much it cost. The first clear routes were written down, so the mail carrier knew exactly where to go.

The mail helped people on a personal level. They could send letters to friends and family who lived far away. Business mail could now go across the country. Important ideas were exchanged that affected history. The revolutionaries sent messages to people to correspond about the War of Independence, and abolitionists sent information protesting slavery.

Eventually, the entire coastal area from Maine down to Florida was connected by the mail system. The mail was still pretty slow compared to our modern experience. But once railroads laid tracks across the nation, the speed picked up even more.

READ

The Telegraph

With our modern phones and email, we often take for granted the ability to communicate with others. Could you imagine it taking weeks or months just to send a message to someone who lives in another state? The **telegraph** was an important invention that started instant communication.

At the time, electricity was just being harnessed to help people. Samuel Morse figured out a way to send beeps of sound across an electrical wire. People could send sounds in a code across far distances instantly. Thousands of miles of telegraph cable were laid across the world.

The telegraph changed how people could live and work. Farmers could receive messages about where their crops were in demand. Business owners could take orders from faraway places. People could send important messages to family members who lived far away, and news events could be told across the country or world instantly.

The telegraph operator listens to sounds and writes them down. The sounds are decoded to form words.

TAKE A CLOSER LOOK

Morse Code

Have you ever heard the famous saying "S-O-S" when someone needs help? If so, you have heard of Morse Code. When the telegraph was invented, it only made sounds similar to a "beep." In order to make these beeps into a code, Samuel Morse invented a system where a long beep was a dash and a short beep was a dot.

Operators sent long strings of dots and dashes that were decoded to form words. So why do we use S.O.S.? The pattern of dot, dot, dot, dash, dash, dash was easy to type if you were in an emergency.

Morse Code

A	•—	M	——	Y	—•——	6	—••••
B	—•••	N	—•	Z	——••	7	——•••
C	—•—•	O	———	Ä	•—•—	8	———••
D	—••	P	•——•	Ö	———•	9	————•
E	•	Q	——•—	Ü	••——	.	•—•—•—
F	••—•	R	•—•	Ch	————	,	——••——
G	——•	S	•••	0	—————	?	••——••
H	••••	T	—	1	•————	!	••——•
I	••	U	••—	2	••———	:	———•••
J	•———	V	•••—	3	•••——	"	•—••—•
K	—•—	W	•——	4	••••—	'	•————•
L	•—••	X	—••—	5	•••••	=	—•••—

It's a Small World

The innovations of the postal system and the telegraph changed the world forever. Many people said that they made the world feel small. They were trying to express a feeling they had—nothing really changed in size. People were using a metaphor. This is figurative language that uses a comparison to make a point or express an idea.

You may have guessed that everyone felt more connected, or maybe that people far away could be contacted much easier. For most of history, people lived in their own small town or village. Many people never traveled more than 10 miles (16 km) away from their homes their entire life. Hardly anyone knew people in other states or countries. Due to the advancements in communication, people could send letters with reliable carriers and send telegraph messages instantly to anywhere in the world! Wow, it is easy to see how people in the 1800s felt like the world had changed.

What do you think people meant when they expressed "the world is getting smaller"?

In this lesson, you learned:

- Communication was slow and unpredictable through most of history.
- The US Postal Service created a more reliable and faster method of carrying the mail.
- Important messages about the Revolution and abolition of slavery are examples of how the mail system changed history.
- The telegraph was the first instant form of communication.

Think About It

What inventions do you use to communicate instantly today?

Circle the correct answer.

1. What did Ben Franklin innovate?

A. the Pony Express

B. a better postal service

C. Morse Code

2. What is a telegraph?

A. the structure needed for railroads

B. the delivery device for letters and mail

C. a system that sends messages across an electric wire

3. What did Samuel Morse contribute?

A. standard measures for the post office

B. a system of dots and dashes for the telegraph

C. safety devices for mail carriers

4. How did the improved post office help change history? Circle all correct answers.

A. Abolitionists sent messages opposed to slavery.

B. Revolutionaries in the 13 colonies could plan to revolt against Britain.

C. The 13 colonies became more connected and unified.

5. Instant access to crop prices is an example of ________.

A. how farmers used the telegraph

B. how bankers made loans with the mail system

C. how factories operated efficiently

Research important developments in the history of communication. Find out when the telegraph, telephone, email, cellular phone, internet, text messaging, and social media were invented. Then plot them on a timeline. Share your timeline with your instructor.

Circle True or False.

6. True or False The Pony Express was an easy way to deliver mail.

7. True or False Ben Franklin was responsible for improving postal delivery.

8. True or False The telegraph transmitted the sound of a voice, just like a phone.

9. True or False Samuel Morse developed a code of dots and dashes.

10. True or False Farmers and business owners benefited from faster communication.

Answer the following question in complete sentences.

11. Explain how the US postal system improved upon older forms of mail delivery.

Lesson 51

Chapter 8 Review

By the end of this lesson, you will:

- review the information from the lessons in Chapter 8, “Growth in the East.”

Lesson Review

Throughout the chapter, we have learned the following big ideas:

- Railroads and canals allowed people and goods to travel between cities faster. (Lesson 47)
- Different ways of life developed in cities and on farms. (Lesson 48)
- Technological advances made eastern cities centers of industry. (Lesson 49)
- Advances such as the postal service and telegraph made communication faster. (Lesson 50)

Go back and review the lessons as needed while you complete the activities.

PLAY

Act out life on a southern farm and in a northeastern city as it was in the 1800s. Use action figures, dolls, or stuffed animals as puppets and perform one scene for each type of life. Make sure to use the vocabulary you have learned in the chapter.

REVIEW

Cities and Farms

The growth of trade, manufacturing, and transportation in the city brought many changes to cities in the North. Cities took on an important role in determining the culture in the North. Merchants, manufacturers, wage earners, and new business owners brought new ideas to city life.

This period of rapid urbanization was known as the Industrial Revolution. The new inventions made city life much different than ever before. There were so many inventions and companies that the United States opened a patent office to protect inventors. They could register their invention on a document. This gave them the right to sell their product or license it to larger companies.

Conversely, the warm climate and fertile soil of the South made it ideal for agriculture to bring about large-scale crops like cotton, rice, and tobacco. Because agriculture was so profitable for southerners, few saw a need for industrial development. Most of the labor force worked on the farm. Many farmers owned a small piece of land and grew crops for their own use. However, there were also plantations. These large farms were controlled by a wealthy owner who made large profits from a single cash crop. Sadly, much of the labor done on plantations was done by enslaved African Americans.

Remember that farming was by far the most common job prior to the 1800s. But what kinds of jobs are more common today? Go online and see if you can learn about the most common jobs today!

Cotton, rice, and tobacco grew well in the South.

Movement and Communication

In the 1800s, waterways called canals became the most important transportation system. They connected smaller waterways to larger bodies of water. Ships could travel and deliver products. Later, railroads were built across the United States. Powerful steam engines moved people and products even faster than canals. Many men were employed, including thousands of Chinese migrant workers who moved to the United States to fill the need for labor. Building railroads was dangerous, hard work.

Industrialists in the Northeast built factories. The first factories produced textiles by weaving cotton. Eventually, all types of products were made quickly and cheaply in large factories. People had access to more products that helped their lives.

Many problems were created as well. Many of the workers were children who could not go to school or have an enjoyable childhood. They worked long hours with dangerous machines. The factories caused pollution. There was not enough housing or services for all the workers who moved to the city. Conditions were unhealthy, and many people died from diseases.

Communication improved across the country. The United States Postal Service was established. It standardized the mail routes and rates to send letters and packages. Inventors made the telegraph, which transmitted electrical beeps across long wires almost instantly. People could send messages in real time to faraway places.

New inventions are often seen as progress. However, there can also be negative side effects of technology. Make sure to note the problems caused by industrialization as you read.

How are canals and railroads similar? How are they different?

PRACTICE

Vocabulary Drawings

Read each vocabulary word below. Then draw a picture that best describes that word.

canal	**textile**
irrigation	**factory**
telegraph	**plantation**

PRACTICE

City Life and Farm Life

In this chapter, we learned that changes in technology changed life for most Americans. This included both farm life and city life. Complete the Venn diagram below to compare similarities and differences between farms and cities in the 1800s.

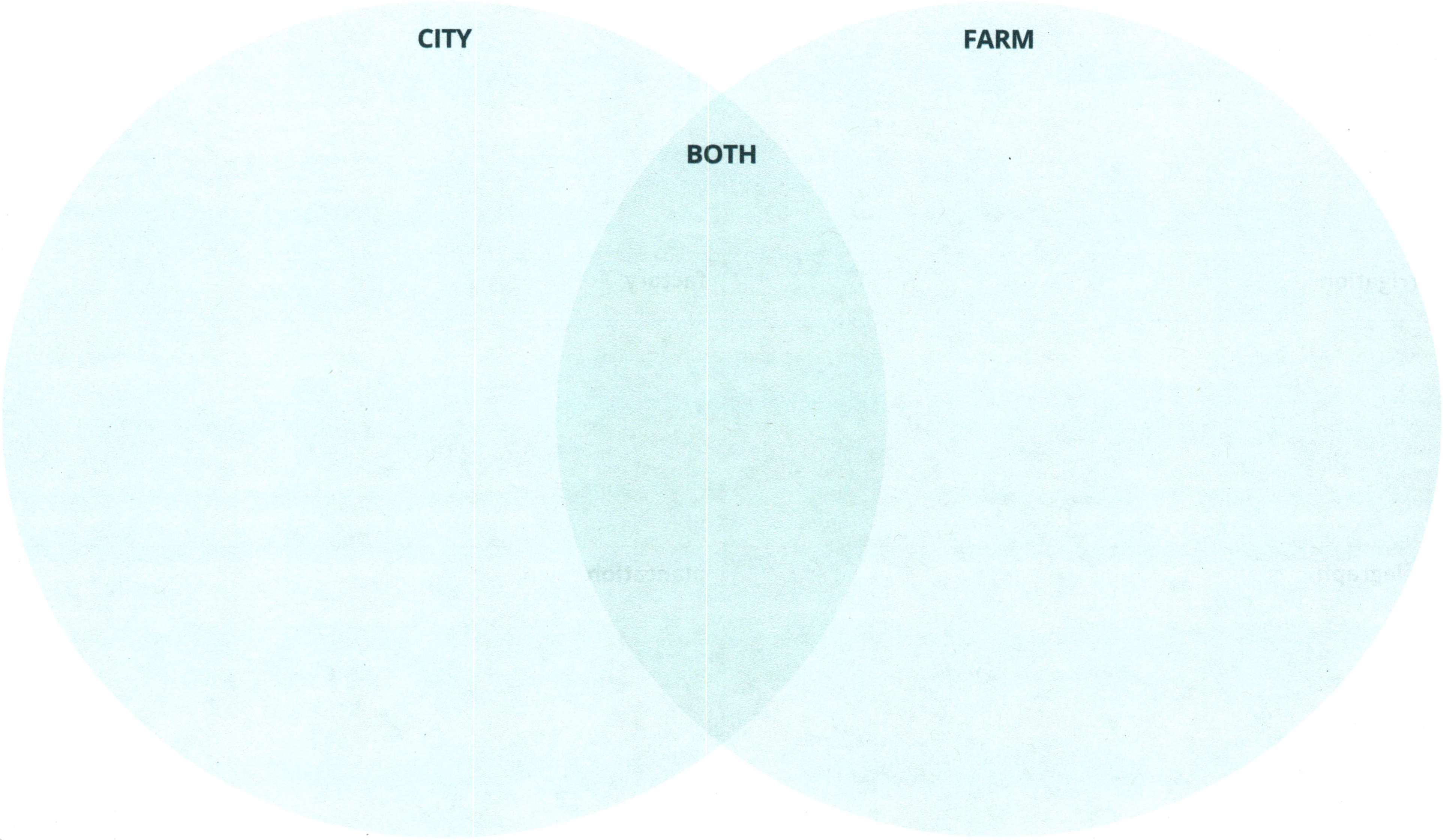

CITY

BOTH

FARM

PRACTICE

Positive and Negative

The rapid advancements in technology brought change to the life of many people during the 1800s. In some ways, these changes were a vast improvement. However, there were also bad consequences. Complete the T-chart below to compare positive and negative outcomes. List three positives and three negatives of industrialization.

EFFECTS OF INDUSTRIALIZATION

Positive	Negative

Think about what you've learned about in this chapter. Circle how you feel:

4 - I know this chapter really well. I could teach it to someone.

3 - I know this chapter pretty well.

2 - I am still learning this chapter. I am not sure about some things.

1 - I am confused. I have a lot of questions about what I've learned.

Talk to your instructor about your answers. When you're ready, ask your instructor for the Show What You Know activity for the chapter.

Chapter 9

Expansion West

Hello, my friend! You know who it is, right? Monty!

I was enjoying our train ride so much. One day, I saw a big sign that said, "Welcome to California!" I was so excited. Hollywood! Beaches! I put on my sunglasses and got ready to see the Golden State.

But I was also sad. Our trip west was about to end. There is nothing after California but the Pacific Ocean.

But in the meantime, it was time to explore California. I learned a lot there, and I'm not lyin'!

We saw big cities in California. San Francisco, San Diego, and the biggest of all, Los Angeles. We were going to the beach, and I was in a great mood!

Professor Tibbs said, "Do you know why there are so many people in this state?" I answered, "Sure! The weather is so great!"

But I was wrong. It was gold! In the nineteenth century, people found gold in California, and thousands of people went there to get rich. They were very disappointed. It turned out there wasn't enough gold for everyone.

Maria said, "But then they stayed for the beaches, right?" We all laughed and walked hand in hand on the sand.

I took in the sun because I knew that soon we would be going back east. But I was ready to roar through that trip!

What Will I Learn?

This chapter looks at the most significant historical landmarks of the US expansion westward in the mid-nineteenth century.

Lessons at a Glance

Lesson 52

Texas Independence

By the end of this lesson, you will be able to:

- identify the laws created by Mexico that people in Texas had to follow
- identify the reason that Texans ended up fighting a war against Mexico
- summarize the key points of the agreement for Texas's independence from Mexico

Academic Vocabulary

Read the following vocabulary word and definition. Look through the lesson. Can you find the vocabulary word? Underline the vocabulary word in your lesson. Write the page number of where you found the word in the blanks.

- **Alamo:** a fortress where a small group of Texans fought against the Mexican Army (page ____)

Geography of Texas

Complete online research to find out geographical facts about Texas. Utilize two or more sources to find:

- the location of the five largest cities
- bordering states
- major landforms
- the location of waterways, including the Gulf of Mexico and major rivers

Discuss what you learned with your instructor.

EXPLORE

Located in San Antonio, the Alamo has become a symbol of courage for Texans and others around the world. During the War of Texas Independence, the Mexican Army attacked an old fort known as the **Alamo**. The Mexican forces numbered nearly 2,000 compared to only 180 Texans. The Texans battled to hold the fort for 13 days, but the Mexicans eventually won and no Texans survived.

Their sacrifice was inspirational for the rest of the Texan forces. Leaders brought troops into battle with cries of "Remember the Alamo."

The Alamo is a popular tourist attraction that draws many visitors each year.

WRITE

Why do you think people were willing to take part in such a dangerous battle?

READ 

Settling in Texas

In the early 1800s, the area we know now as the state of Texas was part of Mexico. This land was sparsely populated, and Mexico wanted to take advantage of the open spaces and rich soil by filling it with more people. The Mexican government sold large pieces of land to buyers who would settle in Texas. Most of the settlers were from the United States. Businessman Stephen F. Austin owned the most land and brought in many Americans to the territory. The large open plains and excellent soil were an attractive draw to many people.

The new Texans were technically citizens of Mexico. However, American-born Texans now far outnumbered the original Mexican inhabitants. Soon, there were about 20,000 American-born Texans compared to only 4,000 Mexicans. The Mexican leaders feared Texas would become more connected to the United States than Mexico.

In 1830, the Mexican government passed a series of laws aimed at controlling Texas. No more American settlers were allowed in, and all present were asked to follow the Catholic religion. Texans were also forbidden from bringing slaves into the territory to work on the large plantations.

The land between the Nueces and Rio Grande rivers was claimed by Texans and Mexico.

Santa Anna Becomes President

In 1833, Antonio López de Santa Anna was elected President of Mexico. He was a powerful leader and decided to change the way the president ruled Mexico. He canceled the Mexican Constitution and declared himself an all powerful ruler. He would be the President for life, and there were no elections.

This made Texans and many other Mexican citizens fearful and angry. They wanted more freedom to have a say in the government's decisions and wanted the government to mostly leave them alone. Many people in Texas wanted to do something about the situation. The Texans considered an armed rebellion against the Mexican leader.

Santa Anna marched a powerful force into Texas. He wanted to crush the rebellion against his rule. Texas did not have an organized or powerful military. A man named Sam Houston began training soldiers, but they were not much of a match to the Mexican Army.

The first battle occurred at the Alamo. A small group of Texans defended the fort along the border between Texas and the rest of Mexico. Rather than just capture the fort, Santa Anna had a total victory and battled until every last Texan soldier was dead. These brutal killings made people enraged against Santa Anna.

Antonio López de Santa Anna by Manuel Paris is in the public domain.

Why do you think that Texans are proud of the events at the Alamo?

READ

Texas Independence

The residents of Texas knew that they must make a decision. Most Texans wanted freedom, their own land, and revenge from the Alamo. Representatives from all over Texas met and declared their own independence. Texas now considered themselves their own country. It was officially the War of Texas Independence.

Many people thought Texas would never be able to defeat Mexico and prove their independence. However, the Texan soldiers used a fast and surprising attack to gain the advantage. At the city of San Jacinto, the Texans attacked Santa Anna's troops. They scored a victory and even took Santa Anna himself prisoner. Texas became an independent country, flying the famous Lone Star Flag.

PRACTICE

Read each sentence. Circle True or False.

1. True or False Texas was a territory of Mexico.

2. True or False By the 1820s, most residents of Texas were American born.

3. True or False General Santa Anna was loved by Mexicans as a kind and gentle president.

4. True or False The Texans won the battle at the Alamo.

5. True or False At the end of the fighting, Texas was established as its own country.

REVIEW

In this lesson, you learned:

- Texas was part of Spanish and Mexican territory.
- Americans led by Stephen F. Austin moved to Texas in large numbers.
- President Santa Anna marched on Texas to crush a rebellion.
- The Texans defeated the Mexican Army.
- Texas became its own independent country.

Think About It

How do you think this unique history affects how Texans feel about their state today?

Choose the correct answer for each question.

1. By 1830, what group made up most of the Texas population?
   - **A.** Native American tribes
   - **B.** settlers from the United States
   - **C.** French explorers
   - **D.** Mexican officials

2. Which of these laws was seen as a positive by the Texans?
   - **A.** Slavery was banned.
   - **B.** Texans had to become Mexican citizens.
   - **C.** Immigrants to Texas were given large plots of land.
   - **D.** Citizens had to follow the Catholic religion.

3. Why did many people dislike Santa Anna?
   - **A.** He did not balance the budget properly.
   - **B.** He was not patriotic toward Mexico.
   - **C.** His ideas were not well understood.
   - **D.** He gave himself too much power.

4. How did the events at the Alamo affect the war?
   - **A.** Texans wanted revenge.
   - **B.** Mexico won the war.
   - **C.** Sam Houston quit the army.
   - **D.** Texans were afraid to join the fight.

5. What was the importance of the Battle of San Jacinto?
   - **A.** Santa Anna was captured.
   - **B.** Texans won their independence.
   - **C.** It was the last battle of the War of Texas Independence.
   - **D.** All of the above

Answer the following questions in complete sentences.

6. Why did the Mexican government become fearful of the situation in Texas?

....

....

....

....

....

....

....

7. Explain how the events of the Alamo motivated Texans even though they were defeated.

....

....

....

....

....

....

....

Lesson 53

Mexican-American War

By the end of this lesson, you will be able to:

- recognize why the United States wanted to annex California to the country
- identify the main events that led to war between the United States and Mexico
- recognize how advancements in weaponry can provide advantages during a war
- identify the main events during the Mexican-American War that led to the United States' victory

Lesson Review

If you need to review Texas independence, please go to the lesson titled "Texas Independence."

Academic Vocabulary

Read the following vocabulary words and definitions. Look through the lesson. Can you find each vocabulary word? Underline the vocabulary word in your lesson. Write the page number of where you found each word in the blanks.

- **Manifest Destiny:** the belief that the United States had the right to expand to the Pacific Ocean (page ____)
- **Mexican Cession:** a large amount of land given by Mexico to the United States after the Mexican-American War (page ____)

Using a computer, look up the state of California. Which country is this state a part of? Is this state boarding any other country? Has this state's land always been a part of the country it is in today? Make your guesses, and then complete this lesson to find out!

EXPLORE

Do you remember how the original United States was really only the 13 colonies along the east coast? Everyone who lived in the original United States lived only in these 13 colonies. However, as time went on, Americans began to move west. In fact, some people became convinced that it was the destiny of the United States to spread all the way to the Pacific Ocean. At first, this westward expansion happened little by little. Pioneers formed small settlements. Then the United States bought the large mass of land known as the Louisiana Purchase. The United States included much of what we now call the Midwest by 1812.

Even though the expansion to the Pacific was still far off, President James Polk believed in the **Manifest Destiny** of the United States. This belief means that one thinks the United States was a special country and had the right to expand to the Pacific to fulfill its destiny. Look at the image. Polk tried to buy the top half of the land highlighted in yellow, but he was unsuccessful. This brought the United States to the brink of a conflict, which we will learn about in this lesson.

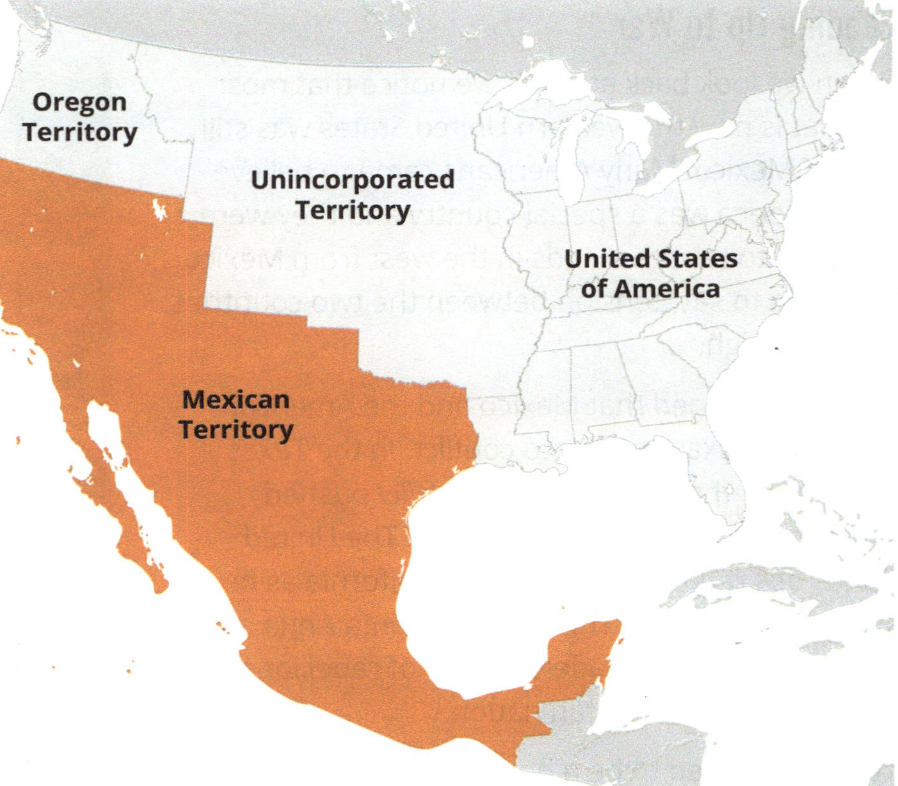

The United States and Mexico around 1845.

What do you think happened when the Americans tried to expand west?

....

....

....

....

Who might have thought that America's westward expansion was a bad idea?

....

....

....

Leading Up to War

When we look back at 1845, we notice that most of what is now the western United States was still part of Mexico. Many Americans came to believe that America was a special country and they were destined to take the lands in the west from Mexico. Needless to say, tension between the two countries was very high.

You have learned that Mexico and the American settlers in Texas came into conflict. In the Texas Revolution, the rebellion successfully pushed President Santa Anna out of Texas. The United States desired to add Texas and California as new states to the Union. This angered Santa Anna and made the Mexican leaders fearful of rebellions all across the large Mexican nation.

Texas continued to be a hotspot of tensions. Many Texans were still very angry at Santa Anna and wanted revenge for the killings at the Alamo. The Texans and the Mexican government had a border dispute. The United States claimed land all the way down to the Rio Grande River. However, Mexico drew the border at the Nueces River. Both Mexico and the Americans built up troops on their sides of the Rio Grande. American President James Polk saw this as the opportunity he wanted to seize control of the West.

READ

The War Begins

America made a fast strike. Troops led by General Zachary Taylor pushed Mexican forces away from the border. The Americans followed and scored victories at the Mexican cities of Palo Alto, Monterrey, and Buena Vista. The Americans won these battles despite having far fewer troops. One reason for the surprising success was superior weapons. Most Mexican soldiers used old leftover British guns. On the other hand, the Americans had the newer Springfield Model 1841 and new Colt revolvers.

At the same time, American settlers in California launched a rebellion against Mexico. They formed an independent country known as the Bear Flag Republic.

Sensing possible victory, President Polk ordered another general—Winfield Scott—to take a second unit of troops deep into Mexico. Scott's troops marched right into Mexico City.

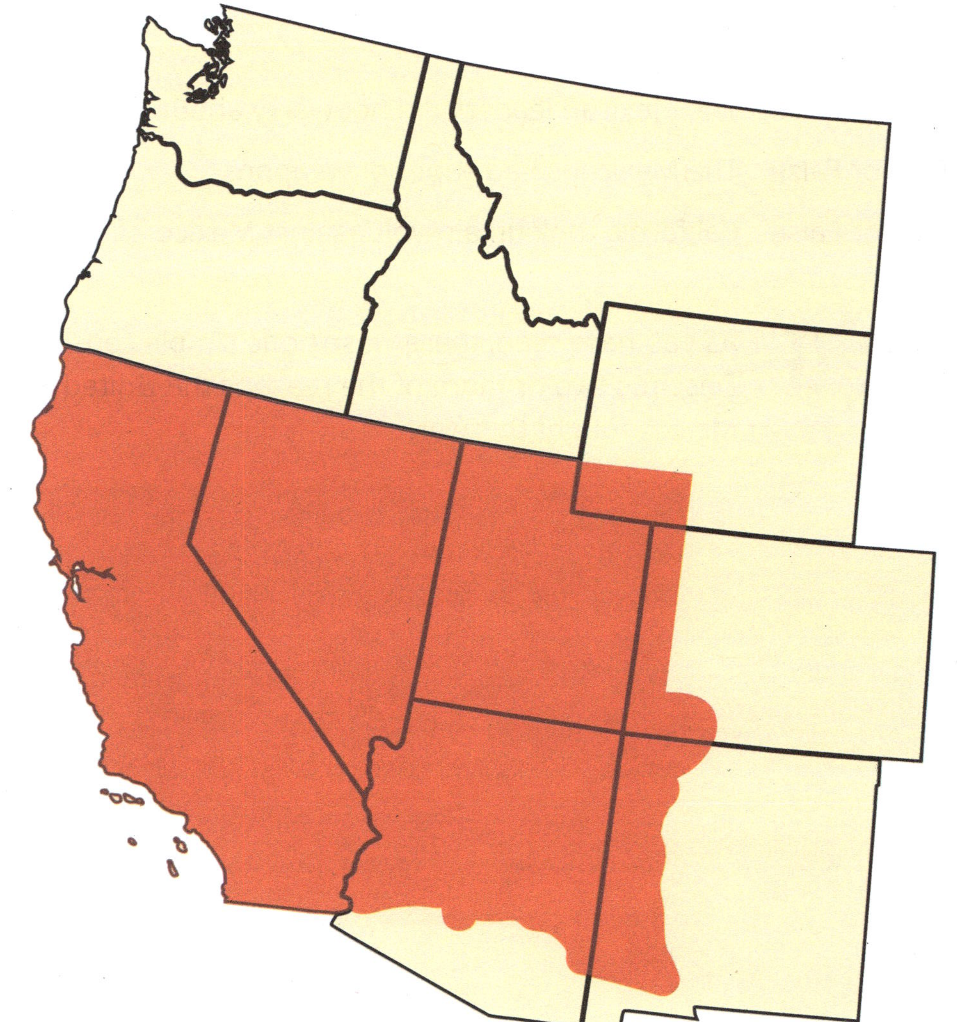

The Mexican Cession included all or parts of California, Nevada, Arizona, New Mexico, and Colorado.

The Mexican Cession

Once the Mexican people saw US troops in control of their own capital, most people were fearful and wanted to surrender. The two countries signed a peace agreement known as the Treaty of Guadalupe Hidalgo. In the treaty, Mexico gave up about half of its land to the United States. The Mexican regions of California, Arizona, New Mexico, Colorado, and Nevada became part of the United States. This transfer of territory was called the **Mexican Cession**. President Polk's mission to fulfill the Manifest Destiny was complete.

PRACTICE

Read each sentence below. Circle True or False.

True or False The Manifest Destiny was a belief that the United States should stretch all the way to the Pacific Ocean.

True or False The Rio Grande River is still the border between Texas and Mexico today.

True or False The Mexican leaders did not worry about rebellions.

True or False The Mexicans had superior weapons.

True or False California took up a revolt against Mexico.

As you have read, there wasn't one simple cause of the war. Describe two or more of the reasons the United States and Mexico fought this war.

....

....

....

....

....

....

....

....

....

....

In this lesson, you learned:

- Many Americans believed that the United States was destined to take over all land between the Atlantic and Pacific Oceans.
- Conflicts between American settlers and Mexico in Texas and California caused tensions between the United States and Mexico.
- The United States used swift attacks and superior weapons to quickly enter Mexico.
- Mexico gave up a large portion of its lands to the United States to end the Mexican-American War.

Think About It

How would the United States be different today if the Mexican-American War had not occurred?

Match each term to its definition.

1. _____ Manifest Destiny	**A.** US General who later became president
2. _____ Mexican Cession	**B.** treaty that ended the Mexican-American War
3. _____ Guadalupe Hidalgo	**C.** river where a border dispute broke out
4. _____ Zachary Taylor	**D.** land given to the United States
5. _____ Rio Grande River	**E.** weapons that helped the Americans win the war
6. _____ Springfield and Colt	**F.** the belief that America should spread to the West

Order the events in which they occurred from 1 (first) to 4 (last).

7. _____ Generals Scott and Taylor won a series of victories in Mexico.

8. _____ Texas already won independence from Mexico.

9. _____ Mexico ceded a large part of its land to the United States.

10. _____ A border dispute broke out around the Rio Grande River.

TAKE A CLOSER LOOK

The Texas border became a source of tension and conflict for many Texans and Mexicans in the 1830s and 1840s. But where do you think the border should have been drawn? Who do you think deserved to own the land between the Rio Grande River and the Nueces River?

Lesson 54

California Gold Rush

By the end of this lesson, you will be able to:

- identify the events that helped cause California's population to greatly increase
- examine how the Gold Rush affected the supply and demand of products in California
- describe how the increase in population affected law and order in California

Lesson Review

If you need to review more about how California became part of US territory, please go to the lesson titled "The Mexican-American War."

Academic Vocabulary

Read the following vocabulary words and definitions. Look through the lesson. Can you find each vocabulary word? Underline the vocabulary word in your lesson. Write the page number of where you found each word in the blanks.

- **Gold Rush:** a rapid movement of people to mine newly found gold (page ____)
- **prospector:** someone who searches for precious metals (page ____)

PLAY

Pretend that you are a miner trying to find gold. Use yellow material such as construction paper to make "gold." Have your instructor or a family member hide the precious metal among other items. Then you can search and find the gold. Imagine the thrill the miners had when they discovered the valuable resource.

EXPLORE

In 1848, a man named James Marshall built a lumber mill on the property owned by John Sutter. While constructing the mill, Marshall found shiny gold flakes and nuggets in the water. It wasn't long before he realized that there was an incredible fortune of gold in the waters, rocks, and dirt of the area. The two men tried to keep the discovery secret. However, the news got out, and by the end of the year, the discovery was known around the country. The California **Gold Rush** would soon begin.

Sutters Mill.jpg by R.H. Vance is in the public domain.

TAKE A CLOSER LOOK

Panning for Gold

Men needed certain equipment to mine for gold. Most commonly, a pick was used to dislodge rock and dirt from a river. Then the loose dirt was shoveled into a special pan. The pan let dirt, tiny rocks, and water drain through, leaving small pieces of gold behind.

Migration to California

California in 1848 was still a remote and sparsely populated land. There were some small tribes of Native Americans and a few thousand former Mexican citizens still living there. The discovery of gold sparked a migration of people from across the United States. Most were young men looking to find a fortune. Thousands of people flooded into California. News of the discovery soon traveled around the world. It did not take long for people from as far away as Europe, Australia, South America, and China to arrive. Soon over 300,000 people entered California.

Many African Americans moved west to California at this time. The territory seemed to hold economic opportunities that were denied to free African Americans in most other places. California was also outside the reach of the federal fugitive slave laws. Enslaved African Americans who had escaped plantations in the South could live in less fear in California than any other place in the United States.

What effect do you think the vast increase in people had in California? Write down two to three difficulties people might face in a territory when so many people move in so fast.

....

....

....

....

....

California Gold Rush relief map 2.jpg by NorCalHistory is in the public domain.

READ

Mining for Gold

Over 300,000 **prospectors** quickly entered California in 1849. Therefore, they are often called "the 49ers." Most were young men hoping to find a fortune. They purchased equipment to mine such as axes, picks, and special pans that could filter the gold. The men formed small temporary towns near a promising stream. Then they staked a claim to the dirt and rock on a small part of the land. Each person sifted through the rock to find some small specks of gold. Sometimes fights broke out over the best areas.

This shift in population was overwhelming. The former Mexican citizens and the native people were vastly outnumbered by the new prospectors. Many of the original inhabitants were forced off their land to make room for the new migrants. Some of the prospectors found gold and became rich. However, many had a difficult time and ended up with little money.

California itself was changed forever by the rapid influx of people and money. Towns began to grow larger, and railroads were built to connect California to the rest of the United States.

miners using equipment to find gold

TAKE A CLOSER LOOK

The Gold Rush in Culture

The Gold Rush was such a big event that many phrases and ideas remain in our culture today. For example, two California sports teams are the San Francisco 49ers and the Golden State Warriors. We use the phrase "struck pay dirt" when we get good fortune that makes money. Pay dirt was the prospectors' nickname for a pile of dirt that held gold.

READ

Law and Order in California

The Gold Rush happened at a time before California had a chance to establish itself as a territory. After the conflict with Mexico, California became United States property. However, there had not been time to establish a strong government or community services. Many of the places that the prospectors settled were just temporary cities with no official government or police force. No one was even sure if Mexican laws still applied or if there were any laws at all.

Adding to the problem, not that many of the prospectors found gold. When someone did find gold, they tried to stake out a claim to the territory. But without laws or law enforcement, it wasn't clear who had the right to any of the land. The prospectors often fought, and violent crimes were common. There were no police or courts to settle conflicts.

This lawlessness pushed Californians to take action. Officials wrote a constitution and law code. They petitioned the United States to join the Union. California was quickly added as a free state.

REVIEW

In this lesson, you learned:

- Gold was found in Sutter's Mill in California.
- Many men migrated to California starting in 1849 to look for gold.
- The Native Americans and former Mexican citizens were treated badly.
- Large amounts of crime resulted because there was no established law.
- California swiftly became a state.

Think About It

How might the entire history of California be different if gold had not been discovered?

Circle the correct answer for each question.

1. Migrants looking for gold started entering California in what year?

A. 1838

B. 1848

C. 1849

D. 1929

2. Where was the gold first discovered that led to the Gold Rush?

A. in an abandoned mine shaft

B. washed up on the beach

C. in the waters outside a lumber mill

D. in Mexican territory

3. Which group moved to California in large numbers? Circle all correct answers.

A. Chinese workers

B. free African Americans

C. Australians, South Americans, and Europeans looking for gold

4. What effect did the Gold Rush have on law and order in California?

A. All the money made theft disappear.

B. There was severe crime.

C. No one knows because records were lost.

D. The powerful Californian government kept crime down.

5. What was the outcome of the territory of California?

A. California was quickly admitted as a free state.

B. No one would allow California to join the Union.

C. California rejoined Mexico.

D. California became a slave state after many years.

6. True or False The California Gold Rush occurred in 1849.

7. True or False Most of the prospectors were native Californians.

8. True or False Most prospectors gained great riches.

9. True or False You did not need equipment to find gold.

10. True or False People migrated to California from all over the world.

Answer the following question in complete sentences.

11. The Gold Rush had both positive and negative effects for different people. Explain two positive and two negative outcomes.

California has a number of museums dedicated to preserving the history of the Gold Rush. Conduct an internet search to discover at least three of the museums. Browse their websites to see images, primary source accounts, and collections.

Lesson 55

Chapter 9 Review

In this lesson, you will

- review the information from the lessons in Chapter 9, "Expansion West."

Lesson Review

Throughout the chapter, we have learned the following big ideas:

- Many Americans moved into the Texas territory controlled by Mexico. War broke out, and the Texans eventually gained independence. (Lesson 52)
- Border disputes between Texans and Mexico later flared up into a larger conflict. The United States won a swift victory in the Mexican-American War. (Lesson 53)
- Mexico gave up large amounts of land to the United States. The California Gold Rush caused a mass migration of prospectors into California. (Lesson 54)

Go back and review the lessons as needed while you complete the activities.

PLAY

Use dolls, action figures, or stuffed animals to act out a scene. Pretend one of the figures is an eyewitness to events at one of the important events detailed in the chapter (like the Alamo, the discovery of gold, or the Treaty of Guadalupe-Hidalgo). The other figure can be a news reporter. Ask questions of the eyewitness, and then have the witness provide answers.

Conflict in Texas

In the middle part of the 1800s, the United States looked to the West. What had once been a country along the eastern coast was rapidly expanding. From 1835 to 1849, several events occurred that changed the history and geography of the nation forever.

In 1835 Mexico battled American settlers in the Texas War for independence. At this time, Texas was still part of Mexico. Thousands of American settlers, led by Stephen F. Austin, moved to the vast open lands of Texas. At the same time, a new President of Mexico was elected. Antonio Lopez de Santa Anna wanted to be an all-powerful leader and called himself President for life. He feared a large number of Americans in Texas might challenge his control. He passed a series of laws that made settlers become Mexican citizens, follow the Catholic religion, and pay more taxes. He banned American settlers from holding slaves.

The Texans organized an army and rebelled against Santa Anna, but the Mexican Army was powerful. In the first battle, Texans tried to defend a fortress known as the Alamo. Not only did Santa Anna defeat the Texans, but his army also killed every single soldier. These killings angered Texans and motivated them to fight even harder. Eventually, the Texas Army defeated the Mexicans and captured Santa Anna. Texas became its own country.

Santa Anna

Santa Anna appointed himself an all-powerful President for life. He disbanded the Mexican Constitution. This made many Mexican citizens upset with him, besides just the Texans. Many citizens dislike it when too much power is given to any one person.

America Expands

The conflict between Texas and Mexico may have ended in 1836, but tensions at the border continued. Mexico and Texas both claimed the land between the Rio Grande and Nueces rivers. Mexican leaders wanted to take back Texas, and Americans wanted to expand into Mexican territory. War broke out at the border. The Mexican-American War raged for two years. The American forces of Zachary Taylor used superior speed and weapons to defeat Mexico in a series of battles quickly. The Americans eventually took the capital of Mexico City.

California was the largest new territory in America. In 1848 and 1849, the new territory gained worldwide attention when gold was discovered. Thousands of people from all over the United States and the world quickly poured into California. Those who searched for gold were called prospectors. There were also many negative effects of the rush of people. Many did not find any gold and had no money to live. The territory was unprepared for so many people, and there was not enough housing or services for all the people. Because there were no effective laws or police force, crime was high, and the situation was dangerous. Soon, California adopted a Constitution and became a U.S. state.

Texas

You may instantly think of Texas as a state in the United States. Remember, Texas went through many different periods of history. Texas was originally inhabited by Native Americans and empires. Spain and France later colonized the territory long before it became part of the United States.

PRACTICE

Three's a Crowd!

For each set of three words, circle the word that does not fit with the others.

1. The Alamo, Nueces River, prospectors
2. Sutter's Mill, Alto California, Rio Grande
3. California, Nevada, Tennessee
4. Zachary Taylor, Winfield Scott, Sutter
5. Prospector, gold, Alamo

When you think about each set of words, decide which two are part of a common event, location, or theme.

Choose two of the word sets above. Write an explanation of how you arrived at the answer. Include what the matching pair had in common and why the third word did not fit.

PRACTICE

Compare Texas and California Settlers

Use the Venn diagram below to compare settlers who moved into Texas and California in the middle 1800s. In addition to differences, use the middle section to show similarities. Think about the following questions: Where did the settlers come from? Why did they move to the new territory? What was their relationship with Mexico?

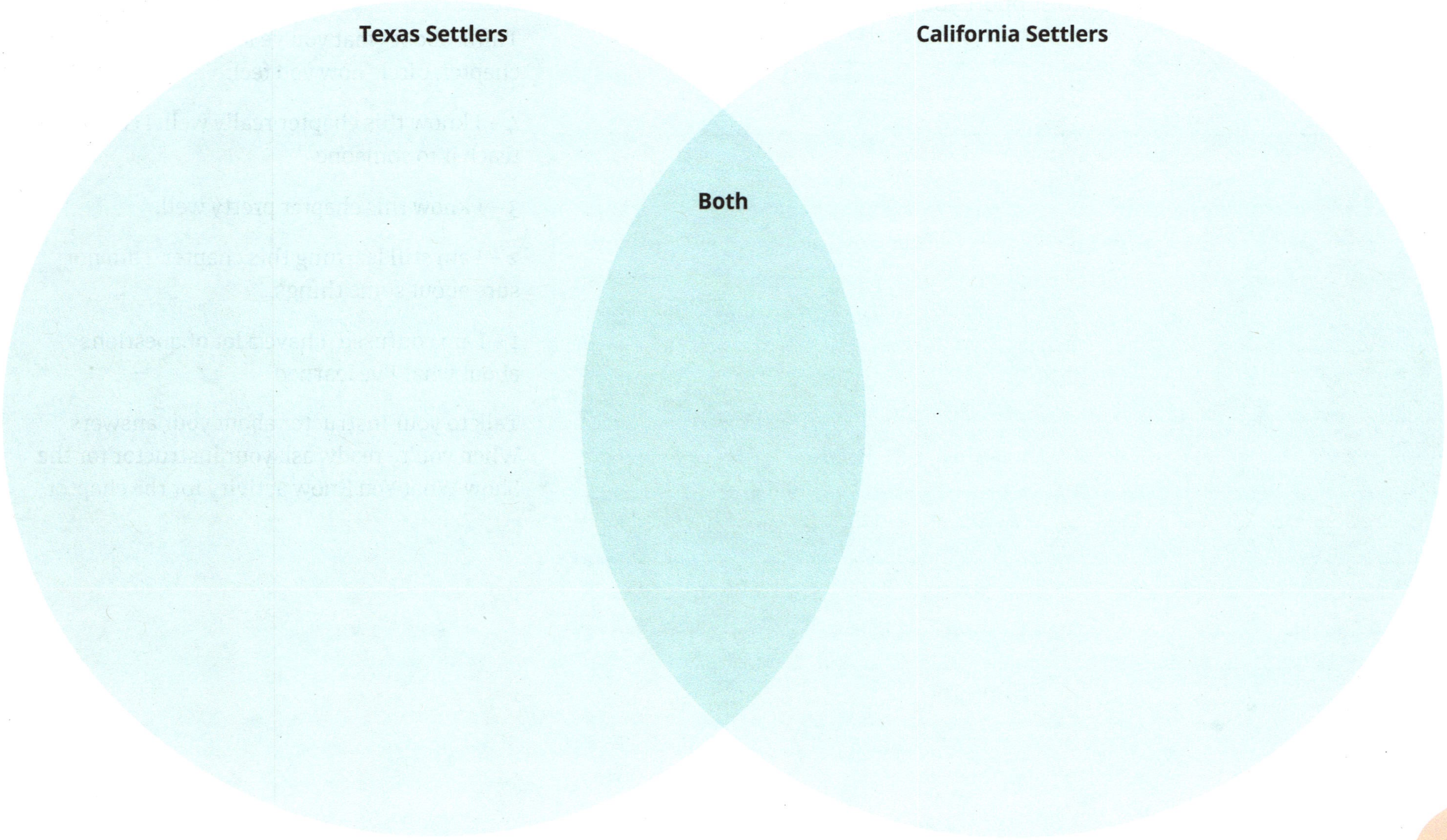

Texas Settlers

Both

California Settlers

PRACTICE

Making an Argument

Evaluate the following claim. Both the United States and Mexico were responsible for the Mexican-American War. Write an argument. In your argument, state whether you agree or disagree with the claim. Use two or more pieces of evidence from the lesson to support your claim.

Think about what you've learned about in this chapter. Circle how you feel:

4 - I know this chapter really well. I could teach it to someone.

3 - I know this chapter pretty well.

2 - I am still learning this chapter. I am not sure about some things.

1 - I am confused. I have a lot of questions about what I've learned.

Talk to your instructor about your answers. When you're ready, ask your instructor for the Show What You Know activity for the chapter.

WRITE

Think about your learning. What stands out to you in the lessons? What questions do you have? What do you wonder about? You can use this page to take notes, write out your responses, and then discuss them with your instructor.

Chapter 10

Slavery

Hello, friend! It is Monty the lion!

The last time I saw you, I was in California with Maria and Professor Tibbs. We decided to head back by car.

Professor Tibbs said, "I teach in the North. You should get to know the South too. Let's drive through that part of the country."

Maria asked, "Is the South very different from the North?" Professor Tibbs nodded and said, "So different that they almost became separate countries!"

I was amazed to hear that. But I wanted to learn all about it.

Let's roar through this!

We were driving through Texas and then on to Arkansas and Mississippi. There were farms everywhere.

Professor Tibbs explained this is part of why the North and the South are so different. In the South, they made money through big farms. However, it is hard to work on a farm, and it doesn't pay that much. In the past, a lot of people in the South made slaves work on their farms.

"That is so sad," Maria said. "Yes," Professor Tibbs said. "Slaves were treated like property instead of people, and they could not run away."

"Didn't they know that was wrong?" I asked. Professor Tibbs replied, "Some people did. That is why there was a war."

I had so many questions that needed answering. But Professor Tibbs said, "We have a long trip and a lot of time to learn!"

What Will I Learn?

This chapter examines the institution of slavery in the United States. In particular, it highlights the role slavery in politics and society.

Lessons at a Glance

Lesson 56

Compromise of 1850

By the end of this lesson, you will be able to:

- compare and contrast the viewpoints and actions of Taylor, Calhoun, and Clay toward the issue of slavery
- identify the creators of the Compromise of 1850
- state the purpose of the Compromise of 1850

Academic Vocabulary

Read the following vocabulary words and definitions. Look through the lesson. Can you find each vocabulary word? Underline the vocabulary word in your lesson. Write the page number of where you found each word in the blanks.

- **compromise:** an agreement to a dispute where both sides agree on the solution (page ____)
- **Congress:** a group of representatives from different states that make decisions for the whole country (page ____)
- **debate:** a structured argument where both sides try to prove that they are correct (page ____)
- **dispute:** a disagreement, argument, or debate (page ____)

PLAY

Most compromises start with a debate. Debates are structured arguments where both sides try to prove that they are correct. Debates occur often in politics before laws are passed or someone new is elected, and they are a way to safely and respectfully argue.

Debates don't always have to be serious. They can also be fun! Start a debate with your family members over what the best dessert is. Can your family come to an agreement over which is the best dessert? Maybe you agree that all types are delicious—that's fine too! There is not always a clear winner in every debate.

EXPLORE

When was the last time you made a compromise? You make compromises with your family, your friends, and even yourself! A **compromise** is an agreement to a dispute where both sides agree on the solution. A **dispute** is a disagreement, argument, or **debate**. Let's look at an example of a compromise.

Mike and Eli are going to walk their dog. They both want to hold the leash. What should they do?

IN THE REAL WORLD

Coming to a compromise is a wonderful way to solve a problem and keep both people happy.

Have a discussion with your family members about important compromises they have made with one another. Hearing examples of compromises other people have made can help you to make compromises of your own.

Circle the situation below that describes a compromise.

1. Mike will hold the leash and Eli will not get to hold the leash.
2. Mike and Eli will fight the whole time over who gets to hold the leash and never take the dog for a walk.
3. Eli will hold the leash and Mike will not get to hold the leash.
4. Eli can hold the leash for the first half of the walk, and Mike can hold the leash for the second half of the walk.

It is not always easy to make a compromise. Some political disputes could affect the lives of all the citizens within a country! When governments make compromises, it takes a long time to come up with a solution where everyone is happy.

How can governments make compromises?

....

....

Does a compromise always resolve a dispute?

....

....

What Was the Compromise of 1850?

The Compromise of 1850 was a series of laws passed by the United States **Congress** in 1850. New Mexico and Utah were new territories acquired from Mexico after the Mexican-American War. California was also seeking to become a state following the Gold Rush. The South wanted slavery to be allowed in the new territories and California, while the North did not.

A compromise was proposed. To make the northerners happy, California would be admitted as a free state, and the slave trade (but not slavery) would be illegal in the District of Columbia. To make the southerners happy, the territories of New Mexico and Utah would be open to slavery by "popular sovereignty," which means they could decide for themselves whether they wanted slaves or not. The Fugitive Slave Act would also become stricter.

It was hoped that the agreement would bring peace over the issue of slavery to the country. However, the American Civil War happened between the North and the South 10 years later.

The Fugitive Slave Act was highly controversial. This act required that slaves be returned to their owners, even if they were in a free state. The act also made the federal government responsible for finding, returning, and trying escaped slaves. This law was an immediate source of tension. Northerners found it very offensive, and many refused to have any part in catching slaves. Some northerners actively and violently obstructed its enforcement. After this law went into effect, the Underground Railroad became more efficient and daring than ever.

READ

Creators of the Compromise

In order to make a compromise that many agreed with, many individuals had to be involved in creating the compromise. Take a look below at the creators of the compromise.

HENRY CLAY

Henry Clay, senator of Kentucky, first created the Compromise of 1850. Clay imagined his bill would be a great compromise between the North and the South. Clay had a two-day speech to persuade the Senate to accept this bill as a compromise between the North and the South.

When Clay offered the initial compromise, it did not go over very well. There was an intense debate within the Senate that lasted for six months without resolution. Clay feared that his idea for a compromise would not pass. Clay turned his proposal over to another senator—Stephen A. Douglas.

Henry Clay

STEPHEN A. DOUGLAS

Stephen A. Douglas, the senator from Illinois, reworked the bill to make it more appealing to both parties. Douglas separated the proposal into five smaller bills that included the following provisions:

1. California was admitted to the Union as a free state.
2. The new territory was divided into New Mexico and Utah, and organized without mention of slavery.
3. The claim of Texas to a portion of New Mexico was satisfied by a payment of $10 million.
4. The Fugitive Slave Act was passed to apprehend runaway slaves and return them to their masters.
5. The buying and selling of slaves was abolished in the District of Columbia, although owning slaves was still permitted.

With the bill split into these new provisions, Congress finally passed the bill, and the Compromise of 1850 went into effect. For the next three years, the compromise seemed to work. Unfortunately, the Compromise of 1850 did not solve all differences.

Stephen A. Douglas

READ

Key Figures

Other key political figures played a major role in the Compromise of 1850. John C. Calhoun, the senator from South Carolina, wanted to expand slavery into the new territories. He did not want California to become a free state and wanted slavery to continue not only in the South but all across the Union. Calhoun defended the slave-plantation system against a growing antislavery movement. In his last address to the Senate, he predicted that a war between the North and the South was likely unless the slave states were given permanent protection to keep slavery alive.

Zachary Taylor was another critical politician in the Compromise of 1850 as he was the president of the United States at the time. Although Taylor was a southerner and a slaveholder himself, Taylor did not push for the expansion of slavery. His strategy as president was to try to keep the peace between the North and the South. Taylor encouraged California and New Mexico to skip the "territory" phase and apply to be a state right away. This helped set the stage for the Compromise of 1850.

PRACTICE

Fill in the blanks to complete each statement.

1. The states in the ________________ wanted the new territory to be free states.
2. States in the ________________ wanted the new territory to be slave states.
3. Slave trade became ________________ in the District of Columbia.
4. ________________ became a free state.
5. The Compromise of 1850 caused the ____________ Slave Act to become stricter.

REVIEW

In this lesson, you learned:

- The Compromise of 1850 was a series of laws about slavery in territories acquired in the Mexican-American War.
- Northerners wanted the new land to be free of slavery while southerners wanted slavery in the new territories.
- Henry Clay came up with the Compromise of 1850.
- Douglas, Calhoun, Taylor, and Seward were important political figures in the Compromise of 1850.

Think About It

Why would the northerners want the new territories to be free from slavery? Why would the southerners want slavery in these new territories? How did political figures' viewpoints on the compromise differ?

Match each politician to their defining characteristics.

1. _____ Henry Clay
2. _____ Zachary Taylor
3. _____ John C. Calhoun
4. _____ Stephen A. Douglas

A. the president of the United States who wanted to keep peace between the North and the South

B. reworked the Compromise of 1850 to make it more appealing and changed the proposal from one large bill to five smaller bills

C. the senator from South Carolina who wanted to expand slavery into the new territories

D. the senator from Kentucky who came up with the idea for the Compromise of 1850

Read each sentence. Circle True or False.

5. True or False The Compromise of 1850 allowed for slave trade within the District of Columbia.

6. True or False Calhoun defended the slave-plantation system against a growing antislavery movement.

7. True or False The Fugitive Slave Act made sure runaway slaves living in free states could remain free.

8. True or False Seward used his position of power to attempt to expand slavery into new territories.

9. True or False Senator Henry Clay first created the Compromise of 1850 as one large bill, but the bill did not pass.

There have been many big compromises throughout history, many involving slavery. Look online to learn more about some of the other compromises listed below.

- The Great Compromise
- Three-Fifths Compromise
- Missouri Compromise
- Second Missouri Compromise
- Crittenden Compromise

Answer the following questions in complete sentences.

10. Describe the viewpoints of the northerners and the southerners during the debates that led up to the Compromise of 1850. What did each side want to see happen?

11. Do you think the Compromise of 1850 was a fair compromise? Why or why not?

Lesson 57

Slavery

By the end of this lesson, you will be able to:

- describe how slaves lived, including their homes and jobs
- describe how slaves were treated in the United States

Lesson Review

If you need to review about slavery, please go to the lesson titled "The Issue of Slavery."

Academic Vocabulary

Read the following vocabulary words and definitions. Look through the lesson. Can you find each vocabulary word? Underline the vocabulary word in your lesson. Write the page number of where you found each word in the blanks.

- **abolitionist:** one who works to end the practice of slavery (page ____)
- **barracks:** a building or group of buildings used to house a large number of people (page ____)
- **Juneteenth:** the celebration of the end of slavery in the United States (page ____)
- **slavery:** the practice of people owning other people (page ____)
- **slaves:** people who are forced to work without being paid and are seen as property (page ____)
- **Underground Railroad:** a network of people who offered shelter and assistance to escaping enslaved people (page ____)

ONLINE CONNECTION

Mount Vernon

Mount Vernon, located in the state of Virginia in the United States, was George Washington's plantation. It was home to George Washington and his family. It was also home to hundreds of enslaved men, women, and children who lived there under George Washington's control. Check out a comprehensive virtual tour of Mount Vernon online.

EXPLRE

What is slavery? **Slavery** is the practice of people owning other people. Enslaved people have to work for their owners, doing whatever the owners ask them to do.

Slavery is part of American history. Enslaved people from Africa were first brought to America in 1619. Americans used **slaves** to do manual labor such as farming, cooking, cleaning, and building. Predominantly, white families owned Black enslaved individuals. They did not view these enslaved individuals as equals. Eventually people realized that slavery was wrong. People called **abolitionists** worked to end slavery. The Northern states made slavery illegal, but the Southern states wanted slavery to continue. The large Southern plantations relied on slave labor. Some enslaved people sought freedom from slavery through a secret organization called the **Underground Railroad**.

Enslaved people chained to one another.

The disagreements over slavery caused the United States to have a war between the North and the South called the Civil War. New laws were created to put an end to slavery. The last slaves were freed on June 19, 1865, which is now celebrated as **Juneteenth**.

TAKE A CLOSER LOK

Solomon Northup

Solomon Northup was a free Black resident of New York who was captured and sold to a dealer of enslaved people. Beaten and chained, he was put on a ship to a New Orleans market and suffered more than a decade of servitude on Louisiana plantations.

Solomon Northup 001 (cropped).jpg by Frederick M. Coffin is in the public domain.

READ

Jobs of Enslaved People

Some enslaved people worked in cities in people's homes or as tradespeople, such as bakers or blacksmiths. However, most lived on plantations. Some enslaved people worked inside the house, and others worked out in the fields. The house servants took care of the house and the family. They cleaned, cooked, did laundry, sewed, and took care of the children of the house. They also cooked and cleaned for the other enslaved people. The enslaved people who worked in the fields were called "field hands." They planted and harvested crops, built and repaired structures, and took care of the livestock. They had to carry heavy things and work in the hot sun.

For enslaved people who worked on plantations, the labor was always hard. They were required to work for as many hours as their bodies would allow. Many would work from sunrise to sunset, only taking short breaks to eat and drink water. Enslaved people did not get paid for their work. They had no choice of jobs and were not allowed to quit. They worked on every day of the week except Sunday. Some enslaved people got days off on Christmas and Easter. Many enslaved people were not allowed to leave the property for fear that they would try to escape.

TAKE A CLOSER LOOK

Frederick Douglass was born into enslavement in 1818 and was raised by his grandmother, who was a slave. Douglass was taken from his grandmother and sold as a slave. He learned to read and write even though it was illegal to educate enslaved individuals. Douglass formed strong opinions on slavery and became disobedient towards his masters. In 1838, Douglass escaped from slavery by disguising himself as a sailor. He went to New York City where he became a well-known abolitionist and wrote a famous book about his time as a slave.

Home Life

The homes of enslaved people, called "slave quarters," were typically constructed of wood and had dirt floors. Those located on large plantations were generally better built, with wooden frames and masonry chimneys and foundations. The most popular houses for enslaved families were one- or two-room structures where all family members slept in the same room. Many enslaved laborers slept where they worked—in kitchens, laundries, and stables.

House servants usually lived in quarters near the owner's house. Enslaved agricultural workers lived in smaller cabins near fields. Slave cabins could be placed single file along a road or randomly distributed as a "slave village." Enslaved individuals who did not have a family were housed in **barracks**, which were rooms with many beds and a small space for each person to store personal items.

In their little free time, enslaved people attempted to exert some free will and choice. Music, storytelling, and religion provided an emotional outlet and carried on traditions—some from Africa and others passed down through years of enslavement. Some people spent their free time visiting other farms or plantations where their spouses or family members lived if they were allowed off of the property.

The inside of a slave cabin.

Slave cabins at Boone Hall Plantation in Mount Pleasant.

Describe what the homes of enslaved people were like.

How Enslaved People Were Treated

Life was not good for enslaved individuals. They did not have basic human rights. They did not have enough to eat, decent places to live, or good clothes to wear. The foods they ate were plain with tiny portions. They would make stews or simple meals out of the ingredients they were given. Enslaved people were given one set of clothing for the year. Their clothes were ragged and stained. They were responsible for mending and washing their own clothing so that they could wear it again the next day. Usually their clothing was made of cheap materials and did not fit well.

Enslaved people were not allowed to learn how to read or write. They could also be sold at any time and separated from their family. Some enslaved people tried to rebel against their owners, but they would be punished and badly treated for disobeying. Slaves in the United States stayed enslaved forever. They could not own any property. Their marriages were not legal, and their families could be broken up at any time. Many people knew that this was not a fair or humane way to treat others. Abolitionists helped enslaved people to escape and become free.

Describe how slaves were treated in the United States.

Harriet Jacobs.jpg by Gilbert Studios is in the public domain.

Harriet Jacobs

Harriet Jacobs was enslaved from her birth in 1813. She was taught to read and write by her enslaver. When her enslaver died, Jacobs was left to a relative who treated her very badly. She escaped and ran to her grandmother's house. For seven years, Jacobs hid in a small space in the attic of her grandmother's home. She became ill from living in confinement, so her family found a sea captain who smuggled her to New York where she lived freely.

PRACTICE

Fill in the chart below with some of the jobs enslaved individuals were responsible for.

House Servants	Field Hands

REVIEW

In this lesson, you learned:

- Slavery is the practice of people owning other people.
- Enslaved people were not treated fairly and did not have basic human rights.
- Enslaved people did not have adequate food, shelter, or clothing.
- All enslaved people worked long hours and had hard jobs, usually as field workers or house servants.

Think About It

Why was slavery immoral? What was life like for enslaved individuals?

Read each sentence. Circle True or False.

1. True or False George Washington owned many slaves on a large plantation called Mount Vernon.

2. True or False Enslaved people work for themselves, doing whatever job they prefer to do in order to earn money.

3. True or False Enslaved people from Africa were brought to America on June 19, which we now celebrate as Juneteenth.

4. True or False People called abolitionists worked to end slavery.

5. True or False Some people were born into slavery and were enslaved for their entire lives.

6. True or False Enslaved people were given one set of clothing for the year. They were responsible for mending and washing their own clothing so that they could wear it again the next day.

ONLINE CONNECTION

Hearing Others' Stories

Reading biographies of enslaved individuals is one way to learn what life was like for these people. Hearing their stories can help you to understand the trauma that enslaved individuals endured. The Library of Congress hosts "Born in Slavery," an online exhibit of interviews from Americans who were once enslaved.

Answer the following question in complete sentences.

7. Choose one enslaved person that you learned about in this lesson and write a summary of their life.

Lesson 58

The Underground Railroad

By the end of this lesson, you will be able to:

- identify possible consequences slaves faced when they ran away
- describe the different experiences of runaway slaves
- name Harriet Tubman as an important conductor of the Underground Railroad

Lesson Review

If you need to review slavery, please go to the lesson titled "Slavery."

Academic Vocabulary

Read the following vocabulary words and definitions. Look through the lesson. Can you find each vocabulary word? Underline the vocabulary word in your lesson. Write the page number of where you found each word in the blanks.

- **abolish:** to stop or get rid of something (page ____)
- **abolitionist:** someone who works to end the practice of slavery (page ____)
- **activism:** an action to make a change within society (page ____)
- **slavery:** the practice of people owning other people (page ____)
- **Underground Railroad:** a network of people who offered shelter and assistance to escaping enslaved people (page ____)

What Kind of Railroad?

Have you ever heard of the Underground Railroad? It was not a train that ran across land on tracks. The Underground Railroad was not actually a railroad. This was a name given to the route many enslaved people took to escape slavery. The term *underground* was used because it was secret, and *railroad* was used because people were being transported to freedom.

EXPLORE

What is activism? **Activism** is when people take action to make a change within society. Many people can be activists, or people who practice activism. Activists can protest, write letters, give speeches, and hold marches to show that they want things to change. Activists take action against climate change, racism, gender discrimination, inequality, and many other political and social issues.

An **abolitionist** is a type of activist who works to end the practice of **slavery**. Many people realized that slavery was wrong and wanted to help enslaved people escape and find freedom. These people wanted to **abolish**—or get rid of—slavery.

Abolitionists worked to help enslaved people find freedom. According to the Fugitive Slave Act of 1850, all escaped slaves had to be captured and returned to their owners, forcing citizens to assist in their return. It was dangerous to be an abolitionist because they were breaking the law, but abolitionists were willing to break the law to help enslaved people find freedom. Some abolitionists built a network of people who all worked together to help enslaved people escape where they lived and find freedom in a new place. This network was called the **Underground Railroad**.

Think of a problem that you would like to see fixed. What problem would you like to fix, and how could you raise awareness about this issue?

CREATE

Think of the problem you identified. Become an activist for this change by taking action. Create a poster or sign to spread awareness of the problem. Research other ways to get involved.

Runaway Slaves

Enslaved people all wanted to be free. They would escape from their slave owners in search of freedom and a better life. No formerly enslaved person ever returned happily to slavery once they found freedom. Every single account of enslaved people who escaped from slavery said that their lives were better as free citizens. Enslaved people ran away to have a chance at a better life.

It was dangerous to try and escape from slavery. Enslaved people were breaking the law by running away. If they got caught, they would be beaten mercilessly, sold back into slavery, or even killed. Many enslaved people were scared to run away for fear of the consequences if they were caught. Many enslaved families were split apart and sold to another plantation if one of them attempted to escape.

Slave owners would put up wanted signs for their runaway slaves, and citizens were responsible for aiding in returning them. If citizens were caught helping slaves run away, they would be charged and punished under the law. Slaves were willing to risk these consequences to find freedom.

$100 REWARD!

Ranaway from Richards' Ferry, Culpeper County, Va., 23rd instant, ABRAM, who is about 30 years old, 5 feet from 8 to 10 inches high, and weighs from 175 to 180. His complexion is dark, though not black, and hair long for a negro. He is a very shrewd fellow, and there is reason to believe he is attempting to get to a free State. I will give the above Reward if taken out of Virginia--$50 if taken 20 miles from home, or $20 if taken in the neighborhood. WM. T. J. RICHARDS,
Adm'r of Jas. Richards, Dec'd.
Sept. 24.

This is a wanted poster for an escaped family of enslaved people.

$100 bounty for runaway slave, Richards' Ferry, VA (cropped).jpg by Wm. T. J. Richards is in the public domain.

What were some of the possible consequences that enslaved people faced if they ran away?

The Underground Railroad

The Underground Railroad was a network of people who offered shelter and assistance to runaway slaves. Many slaves escaped in the middle of the night. They usually ran on foot with not much more than the clothes on their backs and a small knapsack of food. Many slave owners would send out a search party when they realized a slave had escaped. They would use hound dogs to track their scent and have people search on horseback.

It was critical that an enslaved person, upon escaping, had help. Abolitionists would spread the word about safe homes where runaway slaves could hide. These safe homes were part of the Underground Railroad and were called *stations*. The people that would coordinate the assistance to the runaway slaves were called *conductors*. When enslaved individuals ran away, they would head to the nearest station, where they knew they would have shelter and a nice meal. Then the conductors would help them develop a plan for getting them north into a free state. Sometimes they were smuggled onto a boat or train or continued on foot to the next safe house. Sometimes the road to freedom took weeks or months.

Describe the experience of a fugitive slave.

Levi Coffin was a well-known abolitionist and was given the nickname the "President of the Underground Railroad" because of his efforts to assist fugitive slaves. Levi and his wife, Catharine, lived in Indiana. Although the Coffins did not keep records of their abolitionist efforts, it is believed that they assisted over 2,000 enslaved individuals. Their house, known as the Grand Central Station of the Underground Railroad, is now a museum.

Fugitive slaves at the Coffin House, one of the stations of the Underground Railroad.

Levi Coffin House Fountain City Indiana.jpg by Indiana Department of Natural Resources is in the public domain.

READ

Harriet Tubman

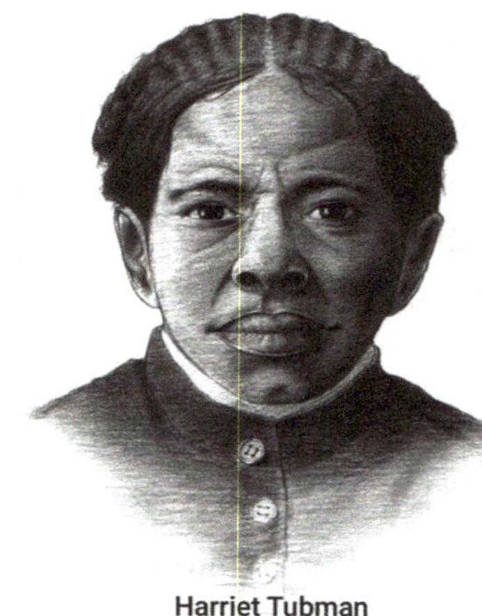
Harriet Tubman

One of the most famous conductors of the Underground Railroad was a formerly enslaved woman by the name of Harriet Tubman. Tubman was born into slavery on a plantation in Maryland. She escaped from slavery in 1849 and committed the next several years of her life to helping other enslaved people escape. As a conductor for the Underground Railroad, Tubman led 19 different trips into Southern states to help over 300 slaves escape. She was never caught and never failed a single mission. Tubman earned the nickname "Moses" because she led her people to freedom like Moses in the Bible.

Tubman was so successful in helping slaves escape that slave owners offered a $40,000 reward for her capture. During the Civil War, Tubman was a nurse to wounded soldiers, served as a spy for the North, and even helped on a mission to rescue over 750 enslaved people. Harriet Tubman bravely risked her own life and freedom to help others.

REVIEW

In this lesson, you learned:

- Abolitionists worked to help enslaved people find freedom.
- The Underground Railroad was a network of people who worked together to help enslaved people escape and become free.
- Slaves were willing to risk the consequences of capture in order to find freedom.
- Harriet Tubman was one of the most famous conductors of the Underground Railroad.

Think About It

Why was becoming a fugitive slave a difficult choice for some enslaved people to make? How did the Underground Railroad assist runaway slaves to find freedom?

PRACTICE

Read each sentence. Circle True or False.

1. True or False Harriet Tubman was born into slavery.
2. True or False Tubman's nickname was "Moses."
3. True or False Tubman worked to find fugitive slaves and return them to their owners.
4. True or False Harriet Tubman was a spy for the North during the Civil War.
5. True or False Harriet Tubman was captured and prosecuted for assisting fugitives.

Circle the correct answer.

1. What was the Underground Railroad?
   - A. a train that took people between the North and the South
   - B. a train system that used underground tunnels
   - C. a network of people and safe houses that assisted enslaved people in their journey to freedom
   - D. a network of people who returned enslaved people back to their owners

2. What is an abolitionist?
   - A. someone who works to end slavery
   - B. someone who works to hunt fugitive slaves
   - C. someone who is a pro-slavery activist
   - D. someone who is against climate change

3. What was the Fugitive Slave Act of 1850?
   - A. a law saying all enslaved people would be freed
   - B. a law stating that all escaped slaves had to be captured and returned to their owners
   - C. a law supporting abolitionist efforts
   - D. none of the above

Many brave people took part in the Underground Railroad. Take a moment to search for these important people who assisted fugitive slaves:

- John Brown and the League of Gileadites
- Charles Torrey
- Reverend Calvin Fairbank
- Captain Jonathan Walker
- John Fairfield
- Frederick Douglass
- Robert Purvis and the Vigilance Committee
- Louis Napoleon
- William Still

4. Which was not a possible consequence that enslaved people faced if they ran away and got caught?

   A. They could be sold and never see their family again.

   B. They could be beaten or punished with violence.

   C. They could be killed.

   D. They could be allowed to remain free.

5. Who was Harriet Tubman?

   A. the owner of the Coffin House, a safe house on the Underground Railroad

   B. a former slave and one of the most famous conductors of the Underground Railroad

   C. a pro-slavery advocate

   D. one of the politicians in the North who advocated against slavery

Answer the following question in complete sentences.

6. Describe how the Underground Railroad assisted runaway slaves and the possible consequences for both the fugitive slaves and the people who helped them.

Lesson 59

Division Over Slavery

By the end of this lesson, you will be able to:

- compare Abraham Lincoln's and Stephen Douglas's views about the issue of slavery leading up to the 1860 election
- describe why Kansas had the nickname "Bleeding Kansas"
- recognize that Americans became more divided over the issue of slavery after the Dred Scott case

Lesson Review

If you need to review slavery, please go to the lesson titled "Slavery."

Academic Vocabulary

Read the following vocabulary word and definition. Look through the lesson. Can you find the vocabulary word? Underline the vocabulary word in your lesson. Write the page number of where you found the word in the blank.

- **emancipation:** freeing a person from slavery (page ____)

Slavery has been present in the world for many centuries. In the United States, enslaved people were brought from African countries. It is a sad truth of human history. The enslavers were often unkind to the people they enslaved. Enslaved people did not make money, have set work hours, or have choices in their work. Enslaved people did rebel, and they rebelled often. Some enslaved people would rebel by creating riots or running away. Other more common rebellions were much smaller. They would slow down their work pace, sabotage crops, and break farming tools.

EXPLRE

Many different people were enslaved. There were laborers, house servants, and nannies. There were enslaved artisans who would practice and learn skills whenever possible. They were dressmakers, blacksmiths, and artists. They formed families, married, had children, and kept those children with them as long as possible. Enslaved people were humans separated from their culture and families, yet they were looked at as property.

It was not just southerners that felt whites were above people of color and the Black communities. This thought was common in Europe and America. Northerners did not want more slave states because they felt it would impact the balance between free states and slave states. That idea is shown in the Missouri Compromise, which you have learned about. Not all white people felt that they were above people of color and the Black communities, but it was commonplace to have these beliefs in the 1800s.

Look at this ad from an auction for the sale of 18 slaves. How were enslaved people viewed based on this advertisement?

TO BE SOLD & LET
BY PUBLIC AUCTION,
On MONDAY the 18th of MAY, 1829,
UNDER THE TREES.
FOR SALE,
THE THREE FOLLOWING
SLAVES,
VIZ.
HANNIBAL, about 30 Years old, an excellent House Servant, of Good Character.
WILLIAM, about 35 Years old, a Labourer.
NANCY, an excellent House Servant and Nurse.
The MEN belonging to "LEECH'S" Estate, and the WOMAN to Mrs. D. SMIT
TO BE LET,
On the usual conditions of the Hirer finding them in Food, Clot in and Medical ance,
THE FOLLOWING
MALE and FEMALE
SLAVES,
ROBERT BAGLEY, about 20 Years old, a good House Servant.
WILLIAM BAGLEY, about 18 Years old, a Labourer.
JOHN ARMS, about 18 Years old.
JACK ANTONIA, about 40 Years old, a Labourer.
PHILIP, an Excellent Fisherman.
HARRY, about 27 Years old, a good House Servant.
LUCY, a Young Woman of good Character, used to House Work and the Nursery.
ELIZA, an Excellent Washerwoman.
CLARA, an Excellent Washerwoman.
FANNY, about 14 Years old, House Servant.
SARAH, about 14 Years old, House Servant.
Also for Sale, at Eleven o'Clock,
Fine Rice, Gram, Paddy, Books, Muslins,
Needles, Pins, Ribbons, &c. &c.
AT ONE O'CLOCK, THAT CELEBRATED ENGLISH HORSE
BLUCHER,
ADDISON PRINTER GOVERNMENT OFFICE.

Slave sale poster.jpg by John Addison is in the public domain.

READ

Views on Slavery

Two men—Abraham Lincoln and Stephen A. Douglas—wanted slavery to end, but they both had opposing views on approaching this big barrier dividing American society. Lincoln wanted to **emancipate**, or free, the enslaved people through federal legislation. He felt that slavery would not stop spreading without legislation outlawing it. Lincoln saw slavery as an evil and maintained that all African Americans should be guaranteed "life, liberty, and the pursuit of happiness."

Douglas wanted the institution of slavery to die out on its own. He felt states should hold the power to decide if they would be free or slave states. Douglas also used the fact that the Constitution of the United States allowed slavery to exist to support his idea that states should be allowed to choose. He believed slavery had to be treated impartially as a public policy question. However, he privately thought it was wrong and hoped it would die out.

Abraham Lincoln

WRITE

What was the difference between Lincoln's and Douglas's views on slavery?

Stephen Douglas

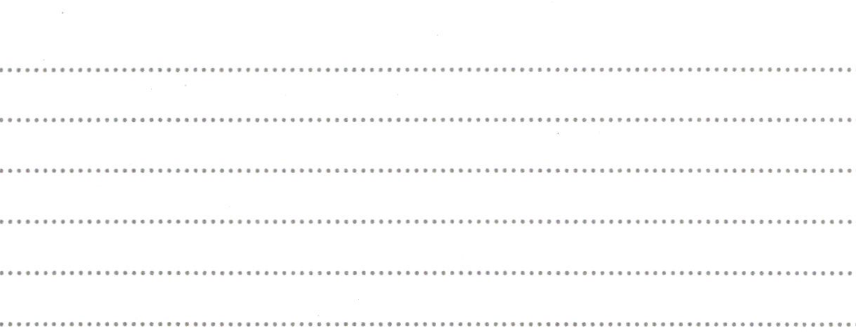

Bleeding Kansas

State of Kansas

Bleeding Kansas is a period of repeated violent disputes after creating the new territory of Kansas in 1854. These conflicts were between pro-slavery and anti-slavery powers. Anti-slavery forces did not like the pro-slavery laws being implemented. The issue of slavery led to an outbreak of guerilla warfare between the two forces in Kansas.

Many settlers who moved to Kansas were midwestern farmers and non-slaveholders from the Upper South. Both groups that had moved to Kansas had little interest in slavery's extension. In contrast, the few pro-slavery settlers were determined to legalize slavery in Kansas. On March 30, 1855, hundreds of heavily armed Missourians came to Kansas and used a loophole as to what constituted "residency" in Kansas to vote in the first territorial election. Consequently, this led to many pro-slavery laws. In response, the anti-slavery force created their own government in Lawrence, Kansas. This split between a pro-slavery government and an anti-slavery government led to violent clashes.

These battles became a prelude to what was to come in the Civil War. Kansas continued to be "Bleeding Kansas" until the Civil War's conclusion in 1865. Bleeding Kansas shaped American politics and contributed to the coming of the Civil War.

What was the main cause of the conflicts that took place in Kansas?

READ

Dred Scott v. Sandford Case

Dred Scott v. Sandford in 1857 was an important decision of the US Supreme Court. The Court maintained that the US Constitution did not intend to include American citizenship for people of African descent, whether enslaved or free. Therefore, any rights provided by the Constitution could not apply to them.

Dred Scott

Posthumous Portrait of Dred Scott by Louis Schultze is in the public domain.

Dred Scott sued for his freedom, claiming that he should be free because he lived on free soil. In 1857, his case was taken to the Supreme Court. There it was ruled that the Constitution did not include African Americans. This decision created a divide in the nation. People who supported slavery celebrated the decision, and anti-slavery people disagreed with the decision. This case further divided the nation over slavery and was one of the many causes of the Civil War.

What were two causes leading to the Civil War?

In this lesson, you learned:

- Lincoln believed that legislation was necessary to end slavery, but Douglas believed that it would eventually die out on its own.
- Conflicts between pro–slavery and anti–slavery groups in "Bleeding Kansas" were one of the causes of the Civil War.
- The Dred Scott case created further division in America.

Think About It

Was Lincoln's approach to ending slavery constitutional? Was this a case to add an amendment to the Constitution?

Match each person with their viewpoint.

1. ______ Lincoln
2. ______ Douglas

A. Slavery was wrong, but the popular influence of Americans should end it.

B. Slavery was wrong, and the federal government had the responsibility to end it.

Choose the correct answer for each question.

3. What does the word *emancipate* mean?
   - A. enslaving people
   - B. freeing a person from slavery
   - C. a debate between two people
   - D. a political process

4. What caused "Bleeding Kansas"?
   - A. a riot of enslaved people against slave owners
   - B. a battle during the Civil War
   - C. emancipation of the enslaved people
   - D. pro-slave laws being implemented in Kansas

5. What was the decision in the Dred Scott case?
   - A. The Constitution protects Americans of African descent.
   - B. The Constitution does not protect Americans of African descent.
   - C. Enslaved people were freed.
   - D. The country would go into a civil war.

Many people of different backgrounds fought for the end of slavery. Also, people experiencing enslavement fought for their rights to freedom. They would commit acts of defiance. Research a person who was enslaved and their efforts to end the institution of slavery. Some people you can research are Frederick Douglass, Nat Turner, and Dred Scott, as well as their families. Find out where they were born and what they did to fight for their freedom and other enslaved people's freedom.

Answer the following question with complete sentences.

6. How did the Dred Scott case create a further divide in America?

....

....

....

....

....

....

....

....

Lesson 60

Points of View

By the end of this lesson, you will be able to:

- compare and contrast Northerners', Southerners', and enslaved people's views of slavery
- summarize what the free states thought about slavery

Lesson Review

If you need to review the divide over slavery, please go to the lesson titled "Division Over Slavery."

Academic Vocabulary

Read the following vocabulary words and definitions. Look through the lesson. Can you find each vocabulary word? Underline the vocabulary word in your lesson. Write the page number of where you found each word in the blanks.

- **abolitionist:** one who works to end the practice of slavery (page ____)
- **antebellum period:** the years from the formation of the Union until the Civil War (page ____)

Throughout the history of the United States, people had different viewpoints, often similar to those in their region. During the division over slavery in the United States, there was a sharp contrast between northern and southern states. Look at the map of the United States in 1861. Slave states were in the South (red) and free states were in the North (blue).

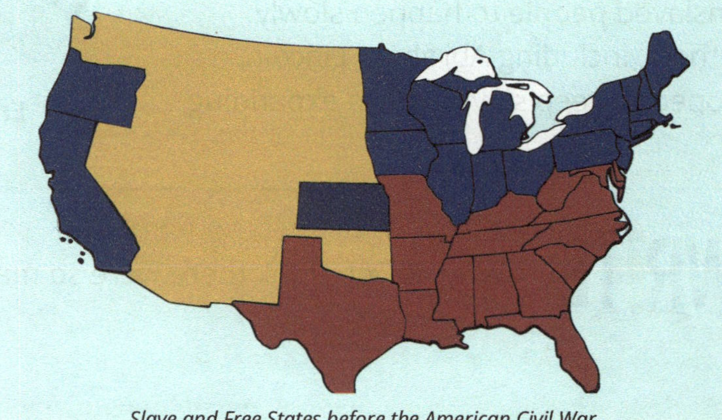

Slave and Free States before the American Civil War. svg by Adam Cuerden is in the public domain.

EXPLORE

We have learned about how the United States became divided over slavery and the differing views in previous lessons. In this lesson, we will continue learning about the different opinions on slavery between the North, South, and people enslaved. Slavery was one of the causes of the Civil War and divide, but not the sole issue. Slavery led to the debate over states' rights and the federal government's role. Some people argued for greater rights for the states, and others argued the federal government needed to have more control. Some people felt slavery was not ok, but states had the right to decide if they would allow slavery. The issue of the continuation of the slavery system fed into this debate of states' rights.

Others saw slavery as morally wrong and felt it should be stopped. However, their views differed on how to end slavery. Some people wanted immediate freedom for all enslaved people, while others wanted the emancipation of enslaved people to happen slowly. Others, including Abraham Lincoln, hoped to keep slavery from expanding.

Enslaved people picking cotton for textiles.

TAKE A CLOSER LOOK

It is important to say "enslaved people" instead of "slaves" when talking about enslaved people. This language separates a person's identity from their circumstance. Having their whole identity labeled as a slave takes away who they are as a whole. It is essential to remember enslaved people did not choose this identity and were forced into these conditions.

WRITE

Why do you think there were so many viewpoints in ending slavery?

Views of Slavery

There were many varying viewpoints on slavery, especially between Northerners, Southerners, and enslaved people. Let's look at each view.

NORTHERNERS

Many Northerners wanted to stop the spread of slavery to keep the political balance between the slave and free states. However, this did not mean they wanted slavery to end ultimately. People profited from cotton that grew in the South, and low income jobholders feared freed enslaved people would take their jobs. But there was a minority of Northerners called abolitionists who were vocal about ending slavery. **Abolitionists** believed slavery was morally wrong and sought to end it.

SOUTHERNERS

Southerners justified slavery by claiming enslaved people were happier than northern wage workers. They viewed the institution of slavery as necessary for America to thrive. Southerners also justified slavery by believing Black people were inferior to White people. Many Northerners held this belief as well.

ENSLAVED PEOPLE

People who experienced slavery worked as laborers in the fields, as craftspeople, or as servants. Many enslaved people longed for freedom but also feared how they would provide for their needs when they were free. The owners of the enslaved people provided shelter and food. Being free also meant no land and the possibility of no work. Even with this obstacle, many enslaved people fought for their freedom.

Abolitionist Movement

Abolitionists focused attention on slavery and made it difficult to ignore. Many abolitionists used religion, such as Christianity, to justify slavery being unchristian. Many White abolitionists focused only on ending slavery. Black Americans also included racial equality in their efforts to end slavery.

How did enslaved people view slavery?

Free States' Views on Slavery

A free state is one where slavery was not allowed. Many free states were in the North. Free states still benefited from slavery. Slavery supplied the labor needed to send cotton to textile mills. The free states profited from the institution of slavery. People in free states did not want slavery to expand to new territories. They wanted the balance to remain the same between free and slave states. In contrast, slave states felt states should have the power to decide if they would allow slavery.

Also, free states saw slavery as wrong, and some believed it needed to end completely. Many free states limited the rights of free African Americans and discouraged migration of more to their states. Even in free states, many White people viewed themselves as superior to Black people and people of color. They didn't want the expansion of slavery but did not want Black people to have the same rights they had.

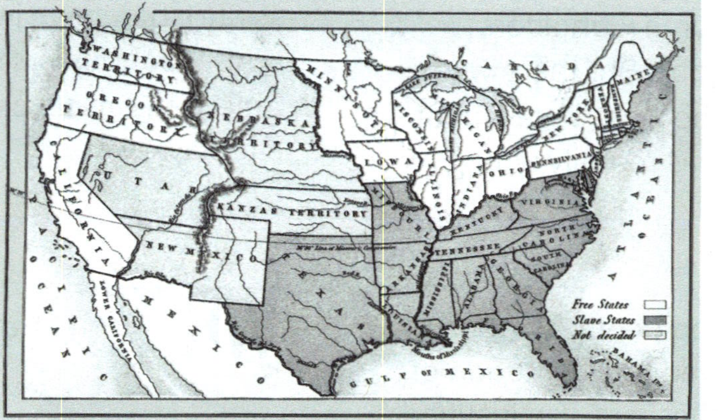

A map of free, slave, and undecided states in 1857.

Life for Freed Black Americans

In the antebellum period, or the years from the formation of the Union until the Civil War, freed Black Americans fought to end slavery. This freedom allowed them to tell their stories and become activists in their communities. They called to end racial injustice and slavery. One example is Olaudah Equiano, who wrote, *An African Captive Tells His Own Story*, that shares a rare look at personal accounts from experiencing slavery.

How did free states view slavery?

PRACTICE

Compare and contrast the views on slavery from the northern states, southern states, and people enslaved. Be sure to include ways their views were similar and ways they were different.

NORTHERNERS	SOUTHERNERS	ENSLAVED PEOPLE

REVIEW

In this lesson, you learned:

- Northerners, Southerners, and enslaved people have or had varying viewpoints about slavery.
- Although they wanted freedom, some enslaved people feared for their survival.
- Many free states differed on the views of slavery.

Think About It

Some people in the South said God intended for Black people to serve them. Does that sound Christian? Why did Christians have different views on slavery during this time?

Choose the correct answer.

1. True or False All Northerners wanted slavery to end.

2. True or False Enslaved people wanted to be free and have racial justice.

3. True or False Both people in the North and enslaved people feared for job opportunities.

4. True or False Free states wanted the immediate freedom of enslaved people.

5. True or False Some abolitionists believed slavery to be unchristian.

6. What period of time is described as the antebellum period?

A. the years during the Civil War

B. the years between the Civil War and the Civil Rights movement

C. the years from the formation of the Union until the Civil War

D. all of the 1800s

7. How did most Northerners view slavery?

A. They did not want the expansion of slavery.

B. They wanted slavery to end in all of the United States.

C. They wanted slavery to expand.

D. They were abolitionists.

Answer the following questions in complete sentences.

8. What were two different viewpoints abolitionists had on ending slavery?

....

....

....

....

9. How did the North and South differ in their views on slavery?

....

....

....

....

10. How did enslaved people view slavery? What was one of their worries about freedom?

....

....

....

....

Lesson 61

Abraham Lincoln

By the end of this lesson, you will be able to:

- describe Abraham Lincoln's positions on slavery
- describe how different groups of people felt about the election of Abraham Lincoln as president
- describe how the Democrats were divided in the election of 1860

Lesson Review

If you need to review the divide over slavery, please go to the lesson titled "Division Over Slavery."

Academic Vocabulary

Read the following vocabulary words and definitions. Look through the lesson. Can you find the vocabulary word? Underline the vocabulary word in your lesson. Write the page number of where you found the word in the blank.

- **Emancipation Proclamation:** the freeing of enslaved people in states that rebelled against the Union in 1863 by Abraham Lincoln (page ____)

Research Abraham Lincoln to create an informational poster or presentation. Include where Lincoln was born, his birthday, when he was president, who his wife was, and three additional facts. Add pictures to illustrate your research.

The statue of Abraham Lincoln inside the Lincoln Memorial.

EXPLORE

Abraham Lincoln was born in the state of Kentucky in 1809. His mother died at a young age, and he was not close to his father. As Lincoln came of age, he became very popular with others. Members of his militia elected Lincoln captain when war broke out between the United States and Native Americans during the Black Hawk War in 1832. This leadership role was the first of many for Lincoln. Following this war, Lincoln went into politics and became a lawyer. In 1860, Lincoln became the 16th President of the United States. His presidency was during a time of division over slavery and states' rights. Lincoln wanted African Americans to have some rights and be free, but his main concern was keeping the Union together. One strategy he used was to issue the **Emancipation Proclamation** in 1863. He freed the slaves in the rebel states and allowed many former slaves to fight for the North. The freed African Americans helped the Union win the war. Lincoln's actions led to the end of the Civil War and the passage of the Thirteenth Amendment to the Constitution banning slavery in all US states and territories.

Abraham Lincoln, the 16th President of the United States.

TAKE A CLOSER LOOK

The Assassination of Lincoln

Many who were in favor of slavery and the rebel movement intensely disliked Lincoln. This included a man named John Wilkes Booth. On April 14, 1865, Booth shot Lincoln and killed him. Lincoln is now remembered for being one of the most influential leaders of the United States during a challenging time in history.

Why was Lincoln important to US history?

Abraham Lincoln's Positions on Slavery

The issue of slavery divided the people in the United States. Many people felt slavery was morally wrong. Others thought it was an important practice. Those in the South relied on enslaved people to work in the fields. Lincoln believed slavery to be morally wrong. He did not want the institution of slavery to expand any further. Lincoln believed people were created with rights, such as the right to liberty. He was antislavery, but he did not free the enslaved people immediately when he became president.

Abraham Lincoln thought slavery was wrong. He believed Black men should have the right to improve their own lives and to prosper. They were equal to white men in that they could improve their lives, making slavery unjust. However, Lincoln did not believe Black people should have the same social and political rights as white people.

Lincoln wanted to end slavery, but admitted he didn't know how to make it happen. Lincoln's first goal was to keep the Union together. Needing more soldiers, he enacted the Emancipation Proclamation. This proclamation allowed more men to fight and help defeat the Confederacy.

Abolitionists and Ending Slavery

Many abolitionists felt slavery should end immediately and that freed enslaved people should be equal members of society. For example, Harriet Beecher Stowe—an American writer, abolitionist, and one of the most influential women of the 19th century—felt protecting enslaved people was more important than working within the political system or under the Constitution. She believed slavery needed to end even if it could not be done within the political system.

How did Lincoln view slavery and Black people?

READ

Public Opinions of Abraham Lincoln as President

Many people agreed with Abraham Lincoln because they believed slavery should end for good. However, not everyone agreed with Abraham Lincoln because many relied on slavery so their plantations could produce crops and make money. Take a look at different opinions of Abraham Lincoln as president of the United States.

THE SOUTH

Many people in the southern states were not happy about Lincoln's election. They knew that Lincoln had an antislavery position. They feared he would try to end slavery and change their way of life. In protest, seven of the southern states decided to leave the Union. This eventually led to the Civil War.

THE NORTH

Northerners were very supportive of Lincoln. Many Northerners opposed slavery and did not want it to expand. Many people in the North supported the Union and Lincoln's antislavery position.

ENSLAVED PEOPLE

Formerly enslaved people supported Lincoln's presidency. They felt Lincoln was the most antislavery presidential candidate. At the same time, Lincoln's antislavery sentiments were lacking to many abolitionists. Lincoln was vocally against slavery, but he made no political effort to outline a plan to emancipate enslaved people during the election or early years of his presidency.

WRITE

What was the criticism about Lincoln's antislavery position from the abolitionists?

TAKE A CLOSER LOOK

Frederick Douglass

Frederick Douglass, a former enslaved person and an abolitionist, once said, "What, then, has been gained to the antislavery cause by the election of Mr. Lincoln? Not much, in itself considered, but very much when viewed in the light of its relations and bearings.... Lincoln's election...has taught the North its strength, and shown the South its weakness...it has demonstrated the possibility of electing, if not an Abolitionist, at least an antislavery reputation to the Presidency of the United States."

Frederick Douglass, "The Late Election," *Douglass' Monthly*, December 1860, from University of Rochester Frederick Douglass Project.

READ

Democratic Party Divide

The Democratic Party was divided during the 1860 election. The people of the Democratic Party had different opinions about who should be their presidential nominee. Slavery was the main issue that led to the split. The party split into the Southern Democrats—who believed slavery should expand to the West—and Northern Democrats—who wanted western territories to decide for themselves if they would permit slavery.

PRACTICE

Using what you have learned in this lesson, draw a picture to show what ideas Abraham Lincoln supported in his run for presidency. Give your drawing a caption with his views on slavery and his main goal as president.

REVIEW

In this lesson, you learned:

- Abraham Lincoln saw slavery as morally wrong and wanted to end it.
- Northerners, Southerners, and enslaved people had differing opinions about Abraham Lincoln's presidency.
- The Democratic Party in the election of 1860 was divided into Northern Democrats and Southern Democrats.

Think About It

Do you think an abolitionist could have won the 1860 presidential election?

Circle the correct answer.

1. What is the main reason Abraham Lincoln was against slavery?
   - **A.** He thought all people should be paid for work.
   - **B.** He believed all people were born with the right to liberty.
   - **C.** He thought slavery would lead to war.
   - **D.** He thought slavery would cost the United States a lot of money.

2. What was the main reason for the divide in the Democratic Party in 1860?
   - **A.** slavery
   - **B.** the economy
   - **C.** states' rights
   - **D.** foreign policy

3. What did the South think of Lincoln's presidency?
   - **A.** They supported Lincoln.
   - **B.** They did not like Lincoln but accepted he won the presidency.
   - **C.** They feared Lincoln would end slavery, so they seceded from the Union.
   - **D.** They were neutral toward Lincoln's presidency.

A Divided Country

Abraham Lincoln once said, "America will never be destroyed from the outside. If we falter and lose our freedoms, it will be because we destroyed ourselves." Lincoln firmly believed in the Union, which is why his main goal was to keep it intact. This is also why he wanted to end slavery within the political system to lessen the divide in the nation. Lincoln felt the divide in the country would destroy it.

4. What criticism about Lincoln's antislavery position did abolitionists have?
   - **A.** they felt he lied and did not want to free the enslaved people
   - **B.** that he did not do enough politically to end slavery
   - **C.** that he went to war over slavery
   - **D.** that he allowed slavery to expand

5. True or False — Lincoln believed Black and white men were politically and socially equal.

6. True or False — Abolitionists wanted freed enslaved people to be equal members of society.

7. True or False — Northerners were very supportive of Lincoln.

Lesson 62

Chapter 10 Review

In this lesson, you will:

- review the information from the lessons in Chapter 10, "Slavery."

Lesson Review

Throughout the chapter, we have learned the following big ideas:

- The Compromise of 1850 was a series of laws determining if territories acquired in the Mexican-American War would be free states or slave states. (Lesson 56)
- Enslaved people were not treated fairly and did not have fundamental human rights. They often had to work long hours without their needs being adequately met. (Lesson 57)
- The Underground Railroad was a network of people that all worked together to help enslaved people escape. Enslaved people risked the consequences of capture. (Lesson 58)
- The United States became divided over slavery with different views from leaders. (Lesson 59)
- Northerners, Southerners, and enslaved people had different views about slavery and abolishing it. (Lesson 60)
- Abraham Lincoln was president during a time of divide in the United States over slavery. This divide led to different opinions of Lincoln's presidency. (Lesson 61)

Go back and review the lessons as needed while you complete the activities.

Enslaved people had to work against their will and often became separated from their loved ones. Their conditions barely met basic human needs, and they were treated as property instead of humans. Enslaved people were not allowed to learn how to read or write, which prevented them from communicating. That means if a family member was sold and separated, they could not write to or read letters from each other.

Compromise of 1850

The Compromise of 1850 was a series of laws passed by the United States Congress over the new territory gained after the Mexican-American War. The North wanted free states, and the South wanted slave states. To make both groups happy, Congress created a compromise. The California territory entered the Union as a free state. The slave trade (but not slavery) also became illegal in the District of Columbia. The territories of New Mexico and Utah would be open to slavery by popular sovereignty, which meant each area could make its own decision.

Slavery

Slavery is the practice of people owning other people. People from Africa were enslaved and brought to colonial America in 1619. Mostly, white families owned Black enslaved individuals. They did not view these enslaved individuals as equals. Enslaved people had different jobs in the field and as servants.

People realized that slavery was wrong. Many former enslaved people and their allies worked to end slavery. They were called abolitionists. The Northern states made slavery illegal, but the Southern states' plantations relied on slave labor and continued the practice.

The Underground Railroad

The Underground Railroad was a way for enslaved people to get help finding freedom. Abolitionists spread the word of safe homes that runaway slaves could go to and hide. If captured, runaway slaves faced severe consequences.

Harriet Tubman

Even though the Underground Railroad was created by a group of abolitionists, many former enslaved individuals—such as Harriet Tubman—used the Underground Railroad to help others find freedom.

Tubman helped over 300 enslaved people escape to freedom. In the Civil War, she was a nurse, a spy for the North, and a helper in rescuing over 750 enslaved people.

Who were abolitionists? What was the Underground Railroad used for?

REVIEW

Points of View

Slavery caused a divide in the United States. Northerners did not want slavery to expand. Southerners felt states should choose to be slave states or free states. Abolitionists and enslaved people wanted slavery to end completely.

The Dred Scott case further divided the nation. The Court maintained that the United States Constitution did not apply to people of African descent. People who supported slavery celebrated the decision, and anti-slavery people disagreed with the decision.

Abraham Lincoln

Slavery was at the forefront of the 1860 presidential election. There was even a split in the Democratic Party because they disagreed on the issue of slavery. Abraham Lincoln did end up winning the 1860 election. The North supported Lincoln, but the South did not. The abolitionists supported Lincoln but felt he could have done more politically to end slavery. In the South, they rejected the presidency, and many Southern states seceded from the Union. This secession furthered the path to Civil War in the United States.

TAKE A CLOSER LOOK

Was Lincoln an Abolitionist?

Lincoln was not an abolitionist. He believed slavery was wrong, but he did not know how to end it. The Constitution did not include the word slavery but did include clauses protecting the institution. Lincoln did not know how to get around the Constitution. Abolitionists did not care about working within the existing political system or under the Constitution. Not until later in his political career did Lincoln fully commit to the abolition movement with the Emancipation Proclamation.

WRITE

Who supported Lincoln's presidency?

PRACTICE

Vocabulary

Use the words below to write a caption for each image.

Word Bank: debate slavery Congress abolitionist activism Emancipation Proclamation

REVIEW

The word *emancipation* in this chapter refers to freeing people from slavery. However, it has a different meaning legally; emancipation is also the process of being set free from legal, social, or political restrictions. Synonyms of empancipation include *liberty*, *freedom*, *liberation*, and *release*. Today, many people in the United States celebrate Juneteenth as the day the news of emancipation reached enslaved people.

PRACTICE

Timeline

Create a timeline of the events leading to Abraham Lincoln's presidency and the South's secession from the Union. Start at the Compromise of 1850. Include a short, two-sentence description of the event or a picture of the event. Include the following events:

1. The 1850 Compromise
2. Bleeding Kansas
3. Dred Scott case
4. The Democratic Party divide
5. The results of the 1860 presidential election

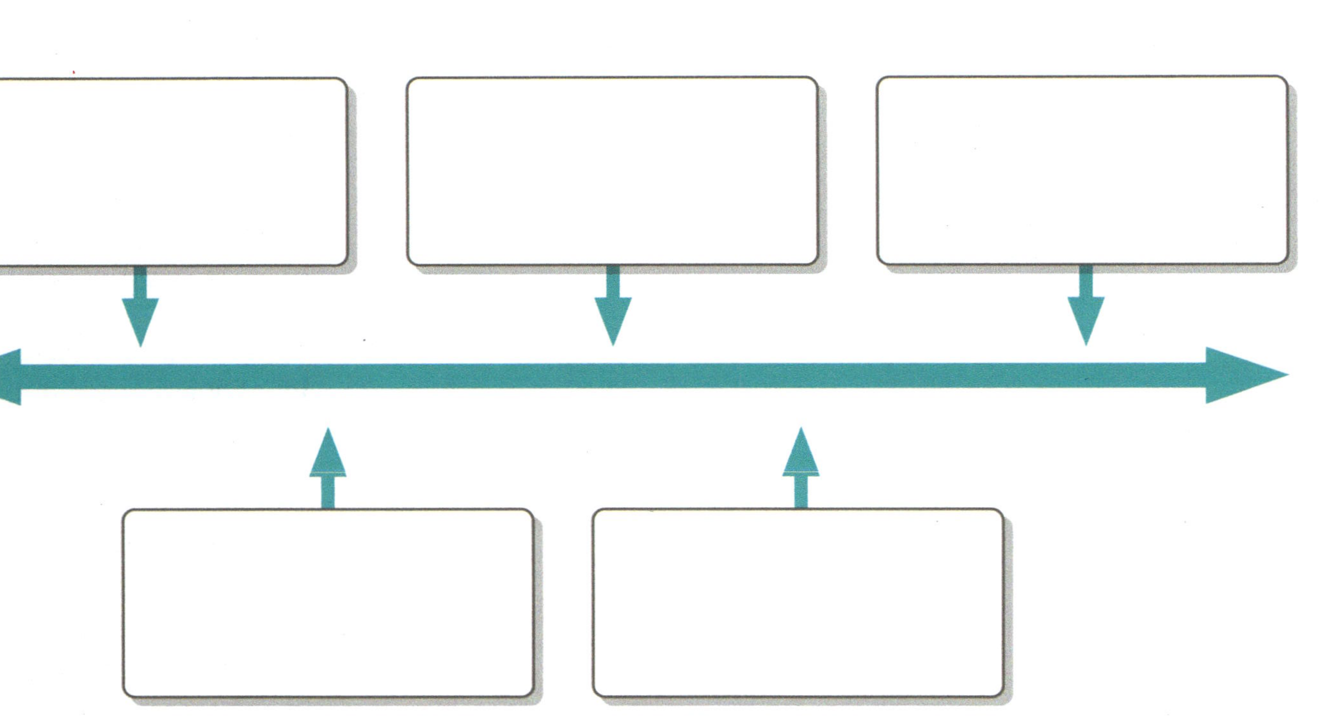

REVIEW

Not all Northerners were abolitionists. Actually, abolitionists were in the minority. It is important to remember that just because a person lived in the North did not mean they wanted emancipation of enslaved people. Most people in the North did not want slavery to expand into new territories. Northerners who worked labored jobs feared the freeing of enslaved people would mean fewer jobs. Wealthy Northerners who owned textile mills benefited from slavery since they received cotton from plantation owners of the South. In contrast, abolitionists saw slavery as inhumane and wanted to end it.

PRACTICE

Points of View Graphic Organizer

Fill out the graphic organizer with the person or group's point of view on slavery.

THE NORTH	THE SOUTH	ENSLAVED PEOPLE	ABRAHAM LINCOLN

Think about what you have learned about in this chapter. Circle how you feel:

4 - I know this chapter really well. I could teach it to someone.

3 - I know this chapter pretty well.

2 - I am still learning this chapter. I am not sure about some things.

1 - I am confused. I have a lot of questions about what I have learned.

Talk to your instructor about your answers. When you are ready, ask your instructor for the Show What You Know activity for the chapter.

WRITE

Think about your learning. What stands out to you in the lessons? What questions do you have? What do you wonder about? You can use this page to take notes, write out your responses, and then discuss them with your instructor.

Chapter 11

The Civil War

Hi, friend! It's Monty again!

We had driven through the South. We met so many amazing people. It was so beautiful. As we started driving back north, the weather changed. It was a bit colder. We saw fewer farms and more factories.

Finally, the car stopped. "Where are we?" I asked. Professor Tibbs said, "Gettysburg, Pennsylvania."

We walked through the open fields of Gettysburg. Here, the Union armies of the North defeated the Confederate armies of the South.

As a future leader, I asked, "How can I make sure my people are never divided like America was?" Professor Tibbs said, "People always disagree. But we need to remember that we have to protect not only our freedom but the freedom of others."

I was reminded of Abraham Lincoln's speech at Gettysburg. He said, "This nation, under God, shall have a new birth of freedom—and that government of the people, by the people, for the people, shall not perish from the earth."

I had to remember to rule for the good and freedom of all. The United States had a war because some people were not free. Learning history is important so we do not repeat past mistakes.

Now I am ready to end this wonderful trip. I hope you enjoyed it as much as I did. I want to hug every one of you!

What Will I Learn?

This chapter examines the US Civil War, how it developed, and how it ended.

Lessons at a Glance

Lesson 63

The Confederate States of America

By the end of this lesson, you will be able to:

- identify the seven states that first joined together to form the Confederate States of America
- describe how West Virginia became its own state

Lesson Review

If you need to review the divide over slavery, please go to the lesson titled "Division Over Slavery."

Academic Vocabulary

Read the following vocabulary words and definitions. Look through the lesson. Can you find each vocabulary word? Underline the vocabulary word in your lesson. Write the page number of where you found each word in the blanks.

- **Confederate States of America:** a group of states that broke away from and fought against the United States in the Civil War from 1861–1865 (page ____)
- **secede:** to formally withdraw from an alliance or union (page ____)

CRETE

Take notes on the lesson as you read. Once you have finished, use your notes and your worktext to create a front-page news story about the founding of the Confederate States of America.

Journalists use language that is simple, clear, and easy to understand. Make sure your writing is easy for anyone to pick up and read. Answer the W questions: Who, What, When, Where, and Why.

EXPLORE

Think about the last time you were on the highway in a car or other vehicle. Were there a lot of other vehicles on the road? Take a look at this picture:

What are some things you notice about this picture that help keep the highway safe and organized?

You may notice the lines between lanes and the divider between the sides of the highway, separating the traffic going in each direction. You may even notice the shoulder where cars can pull over if they have any troubles.

What would happen if a group of people in this city decided they didn't want to follow the rules of the road anymore? What if this group were large enough that whenever people got on the highway, they had to drive with people who didn't want to stay in the correct lane or drive in the appropriate direction? What would that be like? Discuss your thoughts with your instructor.

There was a time when the United States wasn't so united. Some states decided they wanted to do things differently, putting the the future of the Union in jeopardy.

TAKE A CLOSER LOOK

Abraham Lincoln

Think about what you have learned about the election of 1860. Why did Abraham Lincoln win? What were his major positions? What were the opposing opinions? Which states were aligned with Lincoln, and which were against his positions?

Jot down your responses to these questions on a separate paper. As you read, see how your answers relate to what you learn.

The Election of 1860

After Abraham Lincoln won the presidential election in 1860, it became clear that the official policy of the United States moving forward would be to oppose the expansion of slavery into Western Territories. At this time, Inauguration didn't take place in January, but in March (due to the harsh weather in Washington, DC). That left a long time between the election in November of 1860 and Lincoln's Inauguration six months later.

In that time, seven states submitted the necessary documents to **secede** from the United States, or officially withdraw from the nation. They formed their own government and called themselves the **Confederate States of America** (a group of states that broke away from and fought against the United States in the Civil War from 1861–1865).

THE CONFEDERACY

The Confederate government was established on February 8, 1861, just under a month prior to Lincoln's Inauguration on March 4. The oppositional government was considered illegal by the United States. No other country recognized it as a legitimate government.

The seven original members of the Confederacy were South Carolina, Mississippi, Florida, Alabama, Georgia, Louisiana, and Texas. These states are represented in deep red on the map. The light red states would later join the Confederacy once the war began. The yellow states were divided between the Union (represented as blue states) and the Confederacy.

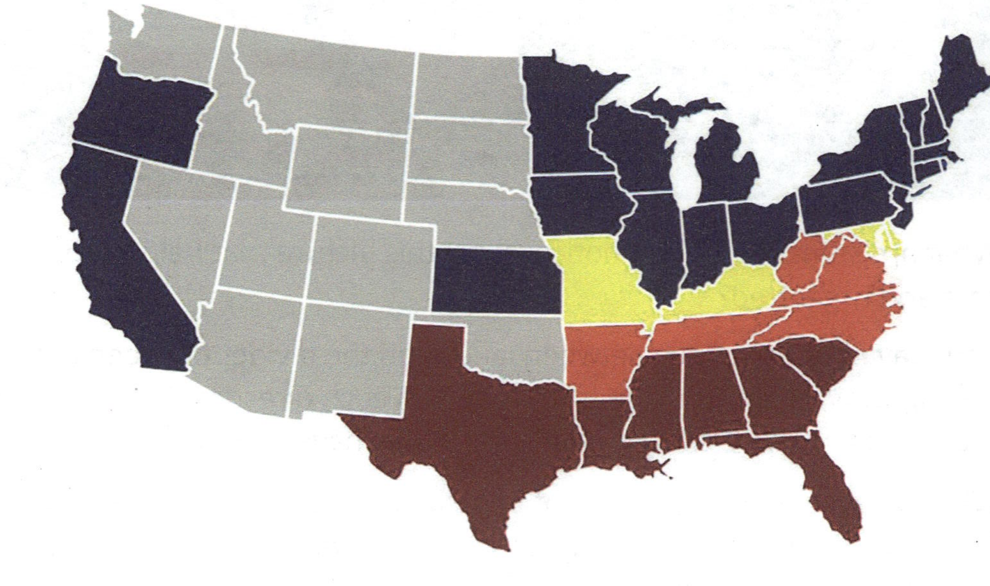

Why did the Confederate states want to secede before Lincoln took office?

Confederate Constitution

The Confederacy drafted its own Constitution, based almost entirely on the US Constitution. However, it did differ in the following ways:

- protected slavery in the Confederacy, allowed the slave trade to continue in the Confederate states, and did not allow anyone to help slaves escape their owners
- limited the government's ability to raise money by eliminating tariffs on imported goods and banning the government from using money raised in one state from funding public works in another state
- money raised by the Confederate government was to support the government, but the U.S. Constitution says that money raised by the U.S. government would be to support the people's welfare
- some states were given more rights, while other states lost some rights (In the Confederacy, the government controlled currency, which is money)

Based on the similarities and differences between constitutions, what did the Confederate States of America find most important?

Stating the Case

Weeks after Lincoln's Inauguration, Confederate Vice President Alexander H. Stephens delivered the Cornerstone Speech explaining the need for secession and forming the Confederacy. He said of the new government:

"Its foundations are laid, its cornerstone rests, upon the great truth that the negro is not equal to the white man; that slavery, subordination to the superior race, is his natural and normal condition. This, our new government, is the first, in the history of the world, based upon this great physical, philosophical, and moral truth."

READ

West Virginia

In the 1820s, tensions between eastern and western Virginians grew over disagreements about government. Western Virginians wanted more democratically elected officials and more of a voice in politics.

Eastern Virginians relied on plantations and slavery to make money.This gave eastern Virginians advantages financially and politically. Even though they counted the full value of property for tax purposes, they only counted enslaved people at a fraction of their worth. They also set requirements for how much property a white man had to own in order to vote. This hurt farmers whose family worked their own land.

After Virginia voted to secede from the Union, a group in the west held a convention to vote on forming a separate state from Virginia. The vote to become a new state passed with a large majority. Many Virginians saw themselves as part of the Confederacy and decided not to vote in any US elections. A state constitution was drafted and revised to meet all requirements to establish a new state—including Lincoln's demand for an abolition clause—and West Virginia was admitted to the Union on June 20, 1863.

PRACTICE

Indicate whether the statements below apply to the Union or the Confederacy.

1. Union or Confederacy — had complete control over currency
2. Union or Confederacy — would not expand slavery into Western Territories
3. Union or Confederacy — accepted West Virginia as a state once it included an abolition clause in its constitution
4. Union or Confederacy — protected slavery by law
5. Union or Confederacy — considered secession and forming an opposing government to be illegal

REVIEW

In this lesson, you learned:

- The southern response to Lincoln's election was secession.
- Originally, seven states seceded. Eventually, eleven states formed the Confederate States of America.
- After Virginia voted to secede and join the Confederacy, a group held a vote to separate into a new state called West Virginia.
- Lincoln accepted West Virginia into the Union after they added an abolition clause to their state constitution.

Think About It

Besides wealth, how did enslavers benefit from owning enslaved people?

SHOW WHAT YOU KNOW

Circle the state in each pair that was an original member of the Confederate States of America.

1. Missouri / Louisiana

2. Maryland / Florida

3. Texas / Kentucky

4. South Carolina / Virginia

5. Alabama / Kansas

6. Ohio / Mississippi

7. Georgia / North Carolina

Answer the following question in complete sentences.

8. Describe how West Virginia became a state.

ONLINE CONNECTION

Research some of the important people of the Confederate States of America. Find out who had each of the following titles:

- President
- Vice President
- General-in-Chief
- Two Cabinet Secretaries
- Two District Judges

Once you have identified important people in the Confederate government, select one to write a one-page biography about and include their role in the Confederacy.

Lesson 64

Battle of Fort Sumter

By the end of this lesson, you will be able to:

- identify states that became a part of the Confederate States of America after the Battle of Fort Sumter
- summarize the main causes of the Battle of Fort Sumter
- identify the main events that occurred during the Battle of Fort Sumter

Lesson Review

If you need to review how the Confederacy formed, please go to the lesson titled "Confederate States of America."

Academic Vocabulary

Read the following vocabulary words and definitions. Look through the lesson. Can you find each vocabulary word? Underline the vocabulary word in your lesson. Write the page number of where you found each word in the blanks.

- **provisional:** existing in the present until changes are made (page ___)
- **sabotage:** deliberately damage (page ___)

CREE

Create a timeline of events beginning with the election of 1860. Start with the election, the dates that the original seven Confederate states seceded, and when they joined the Confederate States of America. You should also include when the provisional constitution (meaning that it would be the constitution temporarily until more changes were made to make it complete) and the official constitution were written.

As you read the lesson, add important events to your timeline. Keep your timeline going to record important events of the Civil War as you progress through the chapter.

EXPLRE

Sometimes people feel like breaking rules or going against someone in a position of authority is okay if the situation calls for it. It can be that they think the person of authority is doing something wrong or harmful. Can you relate?

The Confederate States of America felt like they were forced to take extreme measures against the United States because their rights were being violated. They believed they were going against the United States was acceptable.

Has there ever been a time that you believed that you were right so much that you were willing to risk trouble if you didn't back down? What was that like?

....

....

....

....

....

....

....

....

....

....

....

TAKE A CLOSER LOOK

Making the Right Choice

When you decide to stand up for what you think is right in spite of the consequences, you have to carefully consider the whole situation. Even though you might feel very strongly about something in the moment, it doesn't automatically make you right about it.

How do you know if you're making the right choice? How can you tell when it is time to stand up for your position and when it is time to accept that the other side might be right? Share your ideas with your instructor.

Tensions Increase

After South Carolina seceded in December 1860, the state began seizing, or taking over, federal property that belonged to the U.S. Government within South Carolina. Confederates took over federal buildings, arsenals of weapons, and military forts. In South Carolina, all but two forts had been seized: Fort Moultrie and Fort Sumter.

The U.S. Army placed Major Robert Anderson in charge of Charleston, and initially he and his troops were stationed at Fort Moultrie. The fort was old and designed to shoot outward into the harbor. It was not strong enough to protect against an attack from land.

Knowing he would never be able to defend Fort Moultrie, Major Anderson moved his troops to Fort Sumter in the middle of the night in late December. Fort Sumter was built to be one of the strongest fortresses in the world. It was also positioned at the entrance of Charleston Harbor, a much better strategic position. Before leaving Fort Moultrie, Major Anderson **sabotaged**, or deliberately damaged, the weapons they did not take with them so the Confederate soldiers couldn't take them and use them against the Union soldiers.

Fort Moultrie

Fort Sumter

Why was Fort Sumter a better strategic position for the U.S. Army?

READ

The Point of No Return

Troops at Fort Sumter were running out of food, fuel for heat, and ammunition. President Buchanan attempted to send a relief ship full of supplies. He sent an unarmed merchant ship called the Star of the West. If he sent a naval ship, that would be seen as an act of aggression towards the southern states.

When the ship entered the harbor on January 9, 1861, the Confederates began firing. Major Anderson did not return fire. Following this event, Major Anderson's troops began preparing for war. They strengthened their defenses, positioning 60 guns.

After Lincoln took office, the newly formed Confederacy sent delegates to discuss a peace treaty. President Lincoln refused. If he signed a treaty with the Confederacy, it would make them a legitimate country. On April 4, he authorized another relief mission.

Though neither side wanted to fire the first shots, Confederate President Jefferson Davis told Brigadier General PGT Beauregard to demand surrender once again, or they would fire. Major Anderson refused, and a 34-hour siege began hours later.

Running out of ammunition, Major Anderson ceased fire. A former US Senator watching the battle went to Major Anderson to decide how to end the fight. Major Anderson evacuated his men from the fort on April 13, 1861.

No blood was shed during the battle. However, during a 100-gun salute to the US flag before evacuation, ammunition caught fire and killed two men. They were the first military casualties of the US Civil War.

TAKE A CLOSER LOOK

The newly formed Confederate Army surrounded Fort Sumter. Brigadier General PGT Beauregard stationed men at a series of forts and batteries on Sullivan's Island, Morris Island, and James Island, surrounding Charleston Harbor.

To better understand this battle, review maps of the area to see where soldiers were positioned. Create your own model of the Fort Sumter battlefield. Share your creation with your instructor.

The view across the harbor from Fort Sumter.

READ

War Is Underway

After Fort Sumter, President Lincoln called for 75,000 volunteers to put down the rebellion and recapture the forts. He could only call 75,000 militiamen legally, a number that had been set in 1799 when the US population was one-sixth of what it was in 1861. Due to the Militia Act of 1795, the President was only allowed to ask the soldiers to volunteer for three months out of the year. Congress changed those limits so the men could continue to fight for the Union during the war.

Lincoln sent letters to each governor detailing how many men each state would be expected to recruit. The response across northern Union states was largely an eager one.

The border states did not want to recruit soldiers to fight against their southern "sister states" as Governor Claiborne Jackson said. Border states suggested that Lincoln and the US government were using coercion and acting as tyrants. Because of this, four more states seceded and joined the Confederacy in 1861: Virginia (April 17), Arkansas (May 6), North Carolina (May 20), and Tennessee (June 8).

PRACTICE

Match the person to the conflict or tension they faced.

1. _____ Governor Pickens
2. _____ President Buchanan
3. _____ President Lincoln
4. _____ Governors of Border States

A. couldn't negotiate with Confederate states as that would legitimize their government

B. believed the President had promised not to occupy Fort Sumter

C. wouldn't aid the federal government in what they believed was tyranny against southern states

D. wanted to avoid more states seceding

REVIEW

In this lesson, you learned:

- The United States struggled to maintain order without driving more slave states to secede.
- Lincoln couldn't meet with the Confederacy, but he had to get supplies to the troops, forcing a confrontation between the United States and the South Carolina militia (and later, the Confederate Army).
- No blood was shed during the battle, but two US soldiers died in the evacuation ceremony.
- Virginia, Arkansas, North Carolina, and Tennessee seceded from the Union after Lincoln called for 75,000 volunteer soldiers.

Think About It

How did communication issues make disagreements between parties worse?

Circle the states that seceded following the Battle of Fort Sumter.

1. Texas Virginia Arkansas West Virginia Maryland
   Louisiana Ohio Kansas Missouri Pennsylvania
   North Carolina Tennessee

Circle True or False.

2. True or False During the Battle of Fort Sumter, Major Anderson had to cease fire because the Union troops were running out of ammunition.

Answer the following question in complete sentences.

3. Select at least one cause for the Battle of Fort Sumter and write a detailed explanation of how it led to the conflict.

Imagine if President Lincoln had met with the delegates from the Confederate States of America to negotiate. How would that conversation have gone? Would the outcome have been any different?

Do some additional research on what the Confederate delegates were proposing and what Lincoln's thoughts were in response. Write a script for a play showing what could have taken place if the meeting had happened. Share your play with your instructor or act it out with family and friends.

Lesson 65

The North vs. the South

By the end of this lesson, you will be able to:

- compare and contrast the strengths and weaknesses of the North and the South
- compare the positions of General Robert E. Lee and General Winfield Scott on the war

Lesson Review

If you need to review how the Civil War began, please go to the lesson titled "Fort Sumter."

Academic Vocabulary

Read the following vocabulary words and definitions. Look through the lesson. Can you find each vocabulary word? Underline the vocabulary word in your lesson. Write the page number of where you found each word in the blanks.

- **Anaconda Plan:** Winfield Scott's war strategy to blockade all southern ports and send 80,000 troops down the Mississippi, seizing cities along the way and ending in New Orleans (page ____)
- **brigadier general:** a one-star general who commands a unit, not an entire army (page ____)
- **cohesive:** unified (page ____)

Sometimes people have strong opinions for or against something. The intensity of their feelings on the issue can be surprising. For example, take Hawaiian pizza.

People vigorously defend or criticize the presence of pineapple on pizza. People seem to love or hate it, with little in between. What do you think? Make a list of strengths and weaknesses of Hawaiian pizza. Consult the opinions of others to get more ideas—you might feel too strongly about your opinion to see clearly on this topic!

EXPLRE

People sometimes describe the American Civil War using the phrase "brother against brother". People, even neighbors and families, were bitterly divided over their allegiances.

In the case of Alexander and James Campbell, brothers were literally fighting against each other. The Campbells were immigrants from Scotland. James built a new life in South Carolina, while Alexander moved to New York.

On one occasion, they met on the battlefield but did not know until after. Alexander was the color guard for the Union, displaying the US flag over the battlefield. As the war went on, Alexander wrote to his wife in New York. He said, "It is rather bad to think that we should be fighting, him on the one side and me on the other, for he says he was in the fort during the whole engagement. I hope to God that he and I will get safe through it all and he will have his story to tell about his side and I will have my story to tell about my side."

The two did live through the war. James died in 1907 and Alexander in 1909. They wrote letters through the years and never lost their brotherly love for one another in spite of their opposing sides in war.

TAKE A CLOSER LOOK

James and Alexander Campbell

Can you imagine being in James's and Alexander's shoes during the Civil War? Disagreements with a sibling can be hard enough—but to fight against each other in war with the understanding that each was doing their duty had to have been hard.

How do you think they felt to find out their brother had survived the war? What do you think they wanted to say to each other? Discuss your answers with your instructor.

General Winfield Scott

Winfield Scott was the commanding general of the US Army at the start of the Civil War. Scott was born in Virginia and trained as a lawyer before joining the army at age 22. He served during multiple conflicts, including the War of 1812 and the Mexican-American War. He also ran for president in 1852.

Scott was an advisor to President Lincoln in the beginning of the war. He developed the Union strategy called the **Anaconda Plan**, which was to block all southern US ports and send 80,000 troops down the Mississippi River to capture cities, forcing a final battle at New Orleans.

Many Union generals did not like this plan. They said it was too slow and compared it to an anaconda, a type of snake, wrapping itself around its prey and slowly killing it. The media also criticized the plan. They wanted immediate, aggressive action against the Confederacy. Scott hoped they could cut off the states in the eastern Confederacy from those in the west while keeping the death toll low.

Scott trained and prepared the army to fight, but at age 75, he was too old for the battlefield. President Lincoln ordered Irving McDowell to lead an attack on Richmond, Virginia, agreeing that quick action was needed. The Union suffered a major defeat that was harshly criticized. Scott retired that year and was replaced by George McClellan.

Despite being a Virginian, Winfield Scott stayed loyal to the Union. His formal military dress and strict discipline earned him the nickname "Old Fuss and Feathers." Scott died in 1866. He is considered one of the most accomplished US military generals.

Scott-anaconda.jpg by J.B. Elliott is in the public domain.

READ

General Robert E. Lee

Robert E. Lee became the commanding general during the American Civil War in 1862. Until the Confederate Army formed, state militias fought their own battles. Confederate President Jefferson Davis acted as commander-in-chief, and the branches of the Confederate Army relied on brigadier generals. **Brigadier generals** were one-star generals who commanded units, not the entire army. In the beginning, the Confederate Army had no major generals, and Davis and Brigadier General Joseph E. Johnston planned most of the Confederate strategy. Militias fought throughout the war.

Strategy was not very cohesive because the top of the Confederate military ranks had no coordinated structure. **Cohesive** means unified or organized. In 1862, Lee replaced Johnston. Robert E. Lee also did not have a strategy. He won big victories in southern strongholds by taking big risks. These risks did not always pay off, though. His attempts to invade the North were complete failures. His risky choices and his failure to win victories for the Confederacy led to him being replaced as commander of the Confederate Army in 1864.

One particular strength Lee is noted for is filling positions under him with very talented, skilled soldiers at a time when organization and structure were badly needed.

Robert E. Lee was a desired soldier when the Civil War started. In fact, President Lincoln offered Lee a command in the Union Army! He ultimately remained loyal to the Confederacy.

WRITE

Scott chose the Union despite his Virginia roots, and Lee had his pick of command posts in either army. How does this support and relate to the idea that the Civil War was fought "brother against brother"?

Advantages and Disadvantages

The North seemed to have the clear advantage in the Civil War. They had a much larger population, more states, and an older, more established government that had relationships with other nations. They also had control of almost all manufacturing, including guns and cloth, and transportation. They controlled the US Navy, which could block the import of gunpowder into the South.

However, the North was fighting to keep the southern states as part of the Union. They had to invade, conquer, and fight their own countrymen. The South did have advantages. Their army was the same size, and the morale in the South was high. They felt they were being forced to defend their way of life on their own land. They also had a higher number of experienced generals. The South controlled most food production and forced enslaved people to fight. They melted down metals to make bullets and learned quickly to make their own gunpowder.

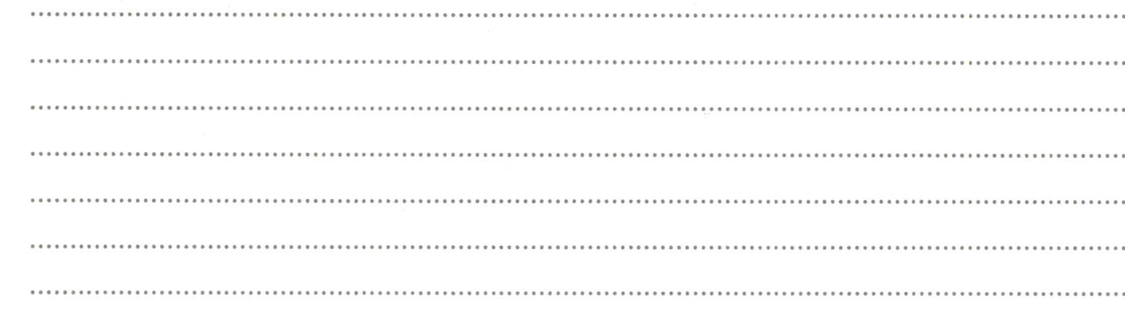

Compare and contrast the strategies and organization of the military in the North and South.

In this lesson, you learned:

- When the Civil War began, General Winfield Scott advised President Lincoln on war strategy. He developed the Anaconda Plan, which was criticized.
- The Confederate Army had to be formed under the new government and operated under President Jefferson Davis, who was commander-in-chief with no major generals.
- Robert E. Lee replaced Joseph Johnston as the brigadier general working most closely with Davis.
- The North and South had distinct advantages in the Civil War.

Think About It

If you were a volunteer soldier at the beginning of the Civil War, what would be your biggest concern on either side?

1. Complete the following T-chart with the advantages each side had in the Civil War.

NORTHERN ADVANTAGES	SOUTHERN ADVANTAGES

2. Which army had the better strategy going into the Civil War?

ONLINE CONNECTION

Research what it was like to be a soldier during the American Civil War. What was life like? What was a normal day for a soldier on either side of the war? Once you have conducted your research, imagine you are a soldier. Write a journal entry describing what life has been like, what you have experienced, and what you expect to happen.

Lesson 66

Civil War

By the end of this lesson, you will be able to:

- identify important Civil War leaders from the North and South
- identify and analyze how early battles and events affected the war

Lesson Review

If you need to review what you learned about the North and South, please go to the lesson titled "The North vs. The South."

Academic Vocabulary

Read the following vocabulary words and definitions. Look through the lesson. Can you find each vocabulary word? Underline the vocabulary word in your lesson. Write the page number of where you found each word in the blanks.

- **appointed:** to assign someone to a position (page ____)
- **demoted:** to be moved down to a lower job position (page ____)
- **fatalities:** soldiers who died (page ____)
- **tactic:** a strategy used to try to win something (page ____)

TAKE A CLOSER LOOK

Civil War Reenactment

Look at the image below. It is a photo of a Civil War reenactment. Describe what you see in this battle. What are both sides doing? How do the soldiers defend themselves? What kind of weapons are they using? Discuss your ideas with your instructor.

EXPLORE

See what you know about the Civil War. Read each statement below and make a guess about each sentence. If you think the sentence is true, circle the number. If you think the sentence is not true, put an X over the number. As you read, you will learn which statements are true.

1. One leader left his strategy plans behind, and they were picked up by the other side.
2. The main battles of the Civil War were the Battle of Fort McHenry and the Battle of Fort Donelson.
3. Ulysses S. Grant was the leader of the Union Army from the beginning to the end of the war.
4. Robert E. Lee and Stonewall Jackson fought for the Confederacy.
5. The Civil War began at Fort Sumter in South Carolina.
6. The Confederate Army did not have a capital or a president.

TAKE A CLOSER LOOK

The US Civil War

Think further about what you know about the Civil War. See if you can answer these questions.

- Why did the Civil War begin?
- What states were involved in the Civil War?
- Do you think there were states that didn't fight for either side?

Discuss your thoughts with your instructor.

Leaders of the Civil War

Throughout the US Civil War, President Abraham Lincoln appointed generals to command the US Army and Navy. **Appointed** means to assign someone to a position. One of those generals was Ulysses S. Grant. At the beginning of the war, Grant led the Army of Tennessee. He won battles at Fort Henry, Fort Donelson, Shiloh, and Vicksburg. At this point, Lincoln appointed him general of the whole army. He was successful in other battles, and he forced a surrender at Appomattox Court House.

Another general for the North was George McClellan. He led the Union Army before Grant. McClellan won some battles, but he always felt that the Confederate Army was larger than the Union Army, so he failed to attack them. Eventually, Lincoln became tired of this and demoted McClellan. **Demoted** means to be moved down to a lower job position.

William Tecumseh Sherman was known for leading the march through Atlanta to the sea. He caused massive destruction along the way. He also assisted Grant at the Battle of Shiloh and Vicksburg.

Robert E. Lee was the leader of the Confederate Army under the established president of the South, Jefferson Davis. Lee had victories at the Second Battle of Bull Run, Fredericksburg, and Chancellorsville. Stonewall Jackson was able to lead armies into battles and was successful in the Valley Campaign. Finally, J.E.B. Stuart fought in major battles, but he caused the loss at Gettysburg due to his mistakes.

Leaders

There were other leaders for both sides that fought in major and minor battles besides the ones mentioned. Others include Joseph Hooker, Winfield Hancock, and George Thomas for the North. Hooker fought in major battles but was demoted shortly after the battles. Hancock was known to have fought at Gettysburg, and Thomas fought in the West. In the Confederacy, Joseph Johnston did not work well with Jefferson Davis. He was a part of many defeats with the Confederate Army.

Who do you think led the Union to victory?

READ

First Battles

The first conflict between the North and the South was at Fort Sumter in South Carolina. It wasn't considered a battle, but it led to the beginning of the Civil War. The conflict began on April 12, 1861, and lasted until the next day. Fort Sumter sits on an island off the coast of South Carolina. The Union soldiers were already at Fort Sumter, with Robert Anderson as their leader. When they refused to leave, General Beauregard's troops fired on them. The Union troops ran low on supplies. Anderson surrendered to the Confederacy. There were no fatalities. **Fatalities** are those soldiers who died.

There were two battles at Bull Run at Manassas, Virginia. One of the first actual battles of the Civil War was the First Battle of Bull Run. The Union marched to Richmond, the Confederate capital. Before getting there, they were confronted by the Confederate troops and fought. It seemed that the Union would win. However, more soldiers came to fight for the Confederacy. During the Second Battle of Bull Run, Stonewall Jackson attacked the Union Army almost a year after the first battle, and the Union lost.

As the Union Army pushed the Confederates south in Tennessee, they met at Shiloh. On the first day of the battle, the Union Army was surprised when the Confederate Army attacked them under the command of General Johnston. Overnight more Union soldiers came to fight. The Confederates were forced to retreat.

Battles

Consider these questions about the battles you read so far:

- Which battle was the best for the Union Army?
- Which battle was the best for the Confederate Army?
- How did the war begin? Did it favor the Union or Confederate Army?

Discuss these questions with your instructor.

Describe what happened during these battles in your own words.

Last Battles

Robert E. Lee had a plan to take over the Union's capital, Washington, D.C. Lee drew up a plan and headed to Maryland. However, he left the plan behind, which was picked up by the Union Army. This allowed the Union Army to know what the Confederacy was up to. After much fighting, Lee and his soldiers escaped. This event was known as the Battle of Antietam.

One of the most famous battles was at Gettysburg. The Confederates could not drive the Union forces back after three days of fighting. On the last day of the battle, the Confederates marched up on Cemetery Ridge, known as Pickett's Charge, but their attack failed. The Confederates were not strong enough to defeat the Union.

One of the final conflicts of the Civil War was the siege of Vicksburg. It was a tactic used to gain the use of the Mississippi River. A **tactic** is a strategy used to try to win something. The Union troops surrounded Vicksburg. As their supplies began to decrease, the Confederacy knew that they would have to give up.

Gettysburg

PRACTICE

Match the name of the leader or battle to its description.

1. ______ Confederate leader who accidentally left his plans behind
2. ______ Leader of the Union Army by the end of the war
3. ______ President of the Confederacy
4. ______ Siege occurred here to secure Mississippi River
5. ______ Union general who was demoted by Lincoln
6. ______ Battle where Pickett's Charge occurred
7. ______ First conflict of the Civil War in South Carolina

A. George McClellan
B. Robert E. Lee
C. Jefferson Davis
D. Gettysburg
E. Vicksburg
F. Fort Sumter
G. Ulysses S. Grant

In this lesson, you learned:

- The main leaders for the Union were President Abraham Lincoln, Ulysses S. Grant, and George McClellan.
- The main leaders for the Confederacy were Robert E. Lee, Stonewall Jackson, and J.E.B. Stuart.
- There were also six major battles or conflicts including Fort Sumter, Shiloh, Antietam, Vicksburg, Gettysburg, and the First and Second Battles of Bull Run.

Think About It

What strategies did the leaders have to win the war?

Fill in the blanks with the correct words from the Word Bank.

Word Bank:	Jefferson Davis	George McClellan	Vicksburg	Antietam
	Stonewall Jackson	Fort Sumter	appointed	Gettysburg
	J.E.B. Stuart	Robert E. Lee		

1. Ulysses S. Grant was ______________________ to his position of general by President Lincoln.

2. The loss of Gettysburg was blamed on ______________________.

3. The first conflict took place at ______________________ off the coast of South Carolina.

4. Wanting control of the Mississippi River, the Union cut off supplies to the Confederacy at ______________________.

5. For the Confederacy, ______________________ led his troops to win at the Second Battle of Bull Run and the Battle of Fredericksburg.

6. The president of the Confederacy was ______________________.

7. Battle plans were found about the strategy to fight at the Battle of ______________________.

8. The Valley Campaign was a victory for the Confederate ______________________.

9. Pickett's Charge was a part of the Battle of ______________________.

10. ______________________ was demoted by President Lincoln because he kept thinking that his troops were outnumbered.

Research further about one of the battles or leaders. Find out through your research the main events of that battle. Discuss what that battle led to and what caused it. If you are researching a leader, describe the leader's education and experience before the Civil War.

Lesson 67

Emancipation Proclamation

By the end of this lesson, you will be able to:

- identify that the Emancipation Proclamation granted freedom to slaves in the Confederacy
- describe how the Emancipation Proclamation impacted the United States
- identify ways Black regiments of soldiers contributed to the war
- recognize that slavery was made illegal in all states by the Thirteenth Amendment

Lesson Review

If you need to review the Civil War, please go to the lesson titled "Civil War."

Academic Vocabulary

Read the following vocabulary words and definitions. Look through the lesson. Can you find each vocabulary word? Underline the vocabulary word in your lesson. Write the page number of where you found each word in the blanks.

- **prohibit:** to stop something from happening (page ___)
- **ratified:** to sign an official document because it is accepted, which makes it valid (page ___)
- **regiment:** a military group (page ___)

Emancipation Proclamation

Many people have heard of the Emancipation Proclamation. What do you think it caused? Who were the people involved in the Emancipation Proclamation? What people were affected by this? Why was this document enacted? Discuss this with your instructor.

EXPLRE

The Civil War was the North against the South. Think about which states sided with the South and which states sided with the North. Some states were not included on either side. These were known as the border states. Shade in the states you think were the southern Confederate states gray, the Union states blue, and the border states green.

Then, think about these questions:

1. Which states were border states?
2. Which states fought for the North?
3. Which states fought for the South?

Discuss these answers with your instructor.

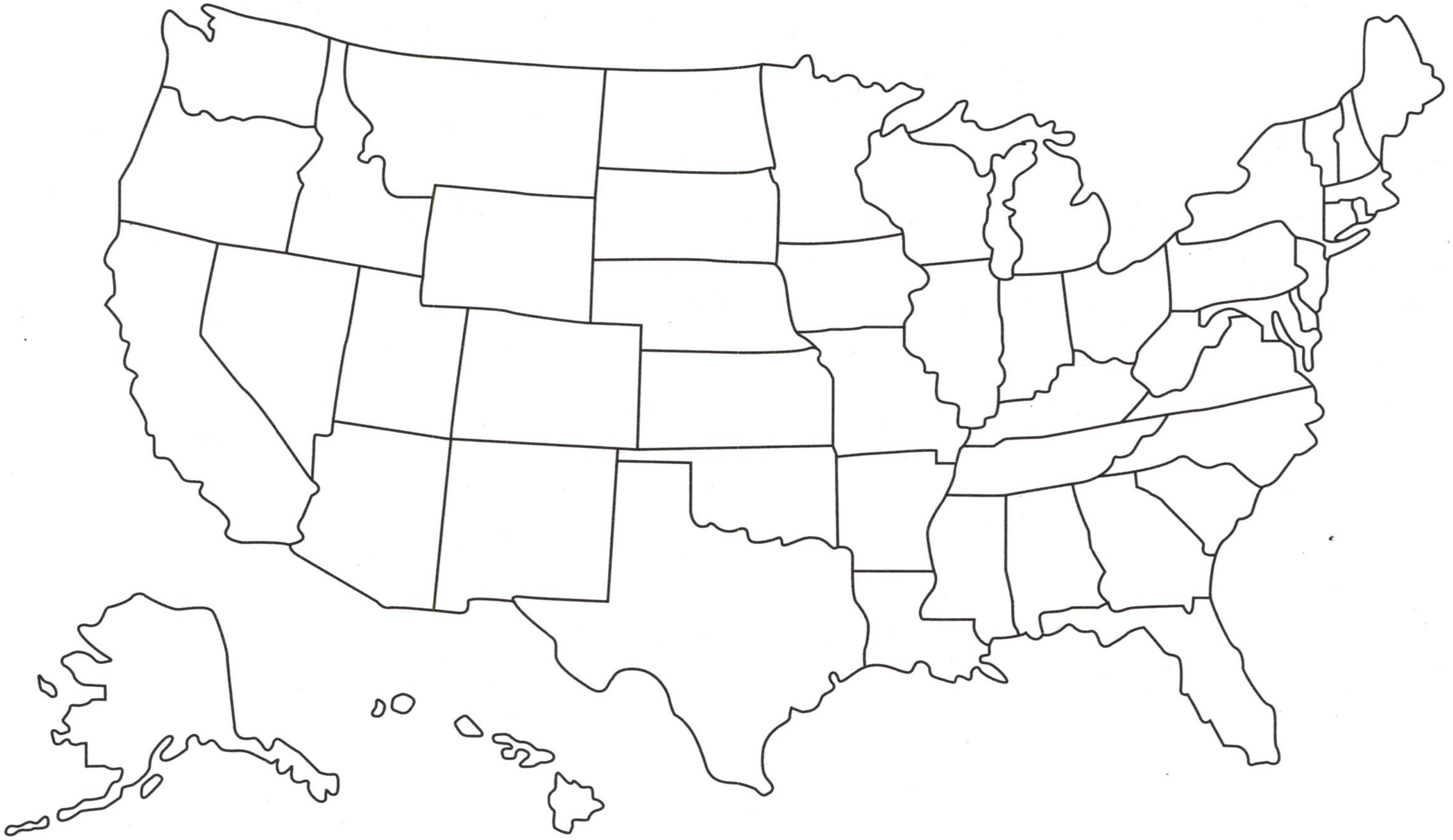

READ

What Is the Emancipation Proclamation?

The Civil War ended on April 9, 1865. However, President Abraham Lincoln issued an order before the end of the Civil War. On January 1, 1863, Abraham Lincoln signed the Emancipation Proclamation. This declared the slaves in the Confederate states free. Many people believe that the Emancipation Proclamation set all slaves free, but that is not the case. Instead, it only freed those who were in states that were part of the Confederacy during the Civil War.

In the United States at that time, there were several million slaves. The Emancipation Proclamation only set 50,000 of the slaves free. It would take two more years before all slaves would be freed. The states that were a part of the Union were not included in the Emancipation Proclamation, and neither were the slaves in the border states.

The Emancipation Proclamation impacted the United States because it would later set the rest of the slaves free in the United States. The Union Army permitted African American soldiers to fight for them. It also paved the way for the adoption of the Thirteenth Amendment, which made slavery illegal.

The Emancipation Proclamation only set the slaves in the Confederate states free.

TAKE A CLOSER LOOK

Sides of the Civil War

There were three groups during the Civil War when you look at the states. A state could be categorized as a state in the Confederacy, Union, or a border state. In the Confederacy, there were 11 states. The Union had 20 states. There were five border states: Missouri, Kentucky, West Virginia, Delaware, and Maryland.

WRITE

What did the Emancipation Proclamation do?

Black Regiments

The Emancipation Proclamation allowed Black soldiers to fight for the Union Army. Before that, the Militia Act of July 1862 first established this right. Almost 200,000 Black men signed up to fight for the Union. By the end of the war, several thousand would receive the status of officer. The Black regiments included former slaves who were free. A **regiment** is a military group. This provided the Union with more soldiers, which was significant in winning certain battles. When the Black soldiers enlisted, they served in combat. Near the end of the war, they would serve in other roles.

The Confederate Army would not allow any Black people to serve in their army. It didn't matter whether they were free or not. There was fear that the slaves would retaliate if they were supplied with weapons to fight in the Civil War. However, near the end of the war, when the Confederacy was losing, they allowed both freed and enslaved men to fight.

The most famous Black regiment was the 54th Massachusetts Volunteer Infantry. They contributed by fighting in many battles. In the middle of July of 1863, they successfully won the Second Battle of Fort Wagner.

Storming Fort Wagner.jpg by Kurz & Allison is in the public domain.

How did the Black regiments contribute to the Civil War?

READ

The Thirteenth Amendment

During the Civil War, the Emancipation Proclamation and the Militia Act of 1862 freed some slaves. It wasn't until the Thirteenth Amendment was enacted that every slave was freed and it became illegal to enslave anyone. Prior to this, the border states and the Union states had no laws that prohibited slavery. To **prohibit** something means to stop something from happening.

Congress passed the Thirteenth Amendment in January 1865, but it took almost a year to ratify it. To **ratify** means to sign an official document because it is accepted, which makes it valid. Every state in the Union at that time had to ratify the amendment in order for it to become a law.

PRACTICE

Answer the questions about the vocabulary.

1. Are children prohibited from driving a car?

2. What kinds of people make up a regiment?

3. If a document is ratified, what does that mean?

4. Could your mom prohibit you from eating sweets before dinner?

5. What would a regiment do?

REVIEW

In this lesson, you learned:

- The Emancipation Proclamation declared slaves in the Confederate states to be free.
- Black regiments like the 54th Massachusetts Volunteer Infantry contributed to the Civil War.
- The Thirteenth Amendment made slavery illegal in the United States.

Think About It

Why do you think the Emancipation Proclamation only included the slaves from the Confederate states?

Read each sentence. Circle True or False.

1. True or False The Black regiments fought throughout the war for both sides.
2. True or False The Emancipation Proclamation freed all slaves in the United States.
3. True or False The Emancipation Proclamation was signed in the middle of the Civil War.
4. True or False It took a year for the Thirteenth Amendment to be ratified.
5. True or False The Thirteenth Amendment freed all slaves in the United States.
6. True or False About 4 million Black men fought in the Civil War.
7. True or False The slaves in the border states were not included in the Emancipation Proclamation.
8. True or False People cannot be jailed because of the Thirteenth Amendment.

Research online for an image of the real Emancipation Proclamation. If possible, look on the National Archives website. Look at the actual document to see how it was written. Look at who signed it and any other information that is on the document. Discuss with your instructor what you learned by looking at the authentic document that was signed.

Lesson 68

Advancements and Inventions

By the end of this lesson, you will be able to:

- describe the improvements and advancements of weaponry during the Civil War
- describe how railroads and telegraphs were used during the Civil War

Lesson Review

If you need to review the Emancipation Proclamation, please go to the lesson titled "Emancipation Proclamation."

Academic Vocabulary

Read the following vocabulary words and definitions. Look through the lesson. Can you find each vocabulary word? Underline the vocabulary word in your lesson. Write the page number of where you found each word in the blanks.

- **bayonet:** a long knife attached to the end of the rifle (page ____)
- **casualties:** the number of soldiers who died in battle (page ____)
- **corps:** a smaller group of a larger military group (page ____)
- **projectile:** a small ball or pellet that is shot out quickly (page ____)
- **reconnaissance:** the examination of areas to find the enemy (page ____)

EXPLRE

Think about what weapons would be used during the Civil War. The Civil War took place between 1861 and 1865, so think about what technology they had back then. That was over 150 years ago. Draw three pictures of weapons that you think soldiers used during the Civil War. Write an explanation of why you chose those weapons.

Improvements in the Civil War

Many inventions and improvements were made during the Civil War to better each side's chances of success. Improvements included the Army Ambulance Corps. A **corps** is a smaller group of a larger military group. Before the creation of the Army Ambulance Corps, wounded soldiers had to wait a long time to get help because they were carried on stretchers to the distant hospital. The Union Army created the Army Ambulance Corps. They were able to place the wounded into the ambulance, which was a horse and a long wagon. It made the evacuation of the wounded from the battlefields run much smoother. As a result, more soldiers survived.

A military strategy that was used by both sides in the Civil War was ballooning. Hot air balloons were not used for sightseeing. Instead, both the Confederate and the Union Armies released hot air balloons for reconnaissance purposes. **Reconnaissance** refers to the examination of areas to find the enemy. When the enemy was spotted, the hot air balloon was used to strike with its artillery.

A third improvement of the Civil War could be found with the Navy's submarines. The Union and Confederate forces both used submarines to block ports. When the area was blocked, the other side could not receive supplies. They were also used as barriers against other Navy warships. Battles were not fought among submarines.

Hot Air Balloons

Hot air balloons were invented and began to be used in the late 1700s. By the time the Civil War occurred in the 1860s, hot air balloons had flown for several decades.

The Union had two main hot air balloons named the *Intrepid* and *Union*. The Confederates had one main hot air balloon called the *Gazelle*. Each traveled at an altitude of 1,000 feet (305 meters) above ground. They could be seen, but sometimes they could hide behind landforms. Five people could fit into the basket of the hot air balloons.

Which improvement do you think was most helpful to the Civil War?

Civil War Weapons

Before the Civil War, common wartime weapons included muzzle-loading rifles and bayonets. A **bayonet** is a long knife attached to the end of the rifle. Moving into the Civil War, technology had advanced, and more weaponry was available. For the first time, the main weapons used were long-range weapons, the Gatling gun, ironclad warships, naval mines, and torpedoes.

The rifled musket was the main weapon used during the Civil War. It still had to be loaded through the musket for each fire, but the pellet was much smaller. This allowed the soldier to shoot faster. Another type of gun was the Gatling gun. The Gatling gun was carried on two wheels. Similar to a machine gun, the Gatling gun could fire 400 pellets or projectiles every minute. A **projectile** is a small ball or pellet that is shot quickly.

The most popular weapons introduced during the Civil War were ironclad warships. Believed at first to be a deadly weapon, the ironclad warships did not help either side during the war. The Confederates' *Merrimack* fought against the Union's *Monitor* in battle. Very little damage was done, and there were no casualties. **Casualties** refer to the number of soldiers who died in battle.

Torpedoes were prominent in the Civil War, but they weren't shot from submarines. Similar to mines, they were placed strategically in the ocean and detonated when the enemy arrived nearby.

Gatling Gun

To get a better idea of the Gatling gun, look at the image below. It shows what the Gatling gun looked like during the Civil War. This weapon had both benefits and drawbacks. Can you think about these benefits and drawbacks?

How was the rifled musket slower compared to the Gatling gun?

READ

Railroad and Telegraph

Railroads and telegraphs were two of the best inventions of the Civil War. They had already been invented by the time the Civil War came around. However, they were improved and expanded to reach more places in both the South and the North.

The railroad was important for both sides. The trains would bring supplies and new soldiers to battles much faster compared to walking or riding horses. Equipment, horses, and medical supplies were also brought by train. Both sides knew how important the railroad was. They laid more tracks during the Civil War to move these supplies to where they were needed. The North had 22,000 miles (35,406 kilometers) of track compared to the South's 9,000 miles (14,484 km). Therefore the North had a much stronger advantage with the movement of supplies.

The telegraph proved just as important as the railroad. Messages needed to be transported to different areas of the country. Leaders had to wire messages. More wires were laid to allow for more access to telegraph messages.

REVIEW

In this lesson, you learned:

- There were many improvements during the Civil War, including weapons like the Gatling gun and the long-range weapons.
- Ironclad warships were introduced in the Civil War.
- The railroad and telegraph helped both sides with messages and supplies.

Think About It

Why do you think these improvements occurred during the Civil War?

PRACTICE

Match the word to its description.

1. _____ a small ball or pellet that is shot out quickly	**A.** bayonet
2. _____ the number of soldiers who died in battle	**B.** casualties
3. _____ a long knife attached to the end of the rifle	**C.** corps
4. _____ the examination of areas to find the enemy	**D.** projectile
5. _____ a smaller group of a larger military group	**E.** reconnaissance

SHOW WHAT YOU KNOW

Match the term with its description.

1. ______ *Monitor*
2. ______ *Merrimack*
3. ______ Gatling gun
4. ______ telegraph
5. ______ railroad
6. ______ rifled musket
7. ______ ballooning
8. ______ Army Ambulance Corps

A. used for locating and firing on the enemy
B. the Confederacy's ironclad warship
C. organized the way to take the wounded to the hospitals
D. used to send messages over wires
E. the Union's ironclad warship
F. main weapon used in battles
G. used for sending supplies and men to battles
H. a gun similar to a machine gun

ONLINE CONNECTION

Research another weapon or technological advancement in the Civil War. A few of those are listed below. Choose one of those or find one on your own. Explain what this advancement did and how it helped the soldiers in the Civil War.

- Photography
- Repeaters
- Minié Ball

Lesson 69

Battles and Strategies

By the end of this lesson, you will be able to:

- recognize the history of the American Red Cross and how the organization helps during times of war
- explain the importance of the Battle of Gettysburg and the Battle of Vicksburg
- evaluate a wartime strategy, such as General Sherman's March to the Sea

Lesson Review

If you need to review how the Confederacy formed, please go to the lesson titled "Confederate States of America."

Academic Vocabulary

Read the following vocabulary words and definitions. Look through the lesson. Can you find each vocabulary word? Underline the vocabulary word in your lesson. Write the page number of where you found each word in the blanks.

- **American Red Cross:** a humanitarian group that gives emergency assistance, disaster relief, and teaches people how to prepare for disasters in the United States (page ____)
- **humanitarian:** a person who works to improve the lives and living conditions of other people (page ____)
- **Yankee:** a nickname for a person born or living in the northern United States (page ____)

Meeting Harriet Tubman

Harriet Tubman, who was born a slave, was famous for her role as a "conductor" of the Underground Railroad in the 1800s. The railroad was a secret network that helped escaped slaves find their way to freedom. By 1857, Tubman had risked her life to free hundreds of enslaved people, including her own parents. She also fought against the Confederates, which were people from the South.

Imagine that you are enslaved and getting ready for your escape to freedom. Along the way, you meet Harriet Tubman, who asks for your help. How would you help her? Write a paragraph describing your experience on a separate piece of paper.

EXPLORE

What comes to your mind when you hear "American Red Cross"? Perhaps you think about a family member who donated or received blood. You may even think about people who help others during natural disasters like earthquakes, tornadoes, and wildfires. The **American Red Cross** is a nonprofit organization that was founded in 1881 by a nurse named Clara Barton. The organization was originally created to provide military support to soldiers during the Civil War. Today, the American Red Cross provides life-saving humanitarian aid to people in distress.

Take a look at these two images of natural disasters. How do you think the American Red Cross provides life-saving aid to people besides donating blood? Write your ideas in the lines below.

Buildings destroyed by an earthquake.

Houses destroyed by a flood.

READ

The American Red Cross

You have learned that the American Red Cross provides life-saving humanitarian aid to people in distress. Today, the organization also provides food, water, shelter, transportation, and medications for victims of natural disasters and war. In addition, the American Red Cross offers first aid and CPR training.

The American Red Cross has had a long history of helping soldiers during wars. In 1898, the American Red Cross aided the United States military for the first time when it provided medical care to soldiers in the Spanish-American War. During World War I, the organization greatly expanded, creating 100 different locations in 1914 and about 4,000 in 1918.

The Red Cross workers also created hospital ships and trains to help soldiers who were injured. The organization recruited over 100,000 nurses during World War II and sent supplies to American soldiers fighting in Europe. After World War II, the American Red Cross created the first national blood donation program in 1948.

An American Red Cross truck from World War II.

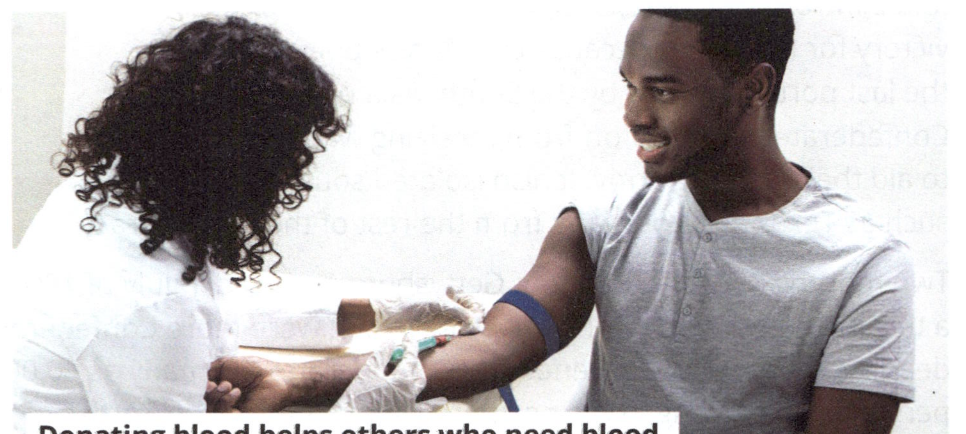
Donating blood helps others who need blood.

WRITE

What kind of assistance did the American Red Cross provide during wars?

The Battles of Vicksburg and Gettysburg

Did you know that the United States was once divided into two sides, the Union and the Confederacy? The North and South had been divided for many years over slavery. President Abraham Lincoln, who governed the Union states, was against slavery and wanted to end it. Many people in the northern states agreed with him, but most people in the southern states did not. This led to the start of the Civil War in 1861. One of the most important battles was the Battle of Vicksburg in May of 1863. During this battle, Union states captured and controlled the Mississippi River. This was a big victory for the Union because the Mississippi River was the last port controlled by the South. As a result, the Confederates were cut off from receiving war supplies to aid their growing army. It also isolated southern states such as Texas and Louisiana from the rest of the Confederacy.

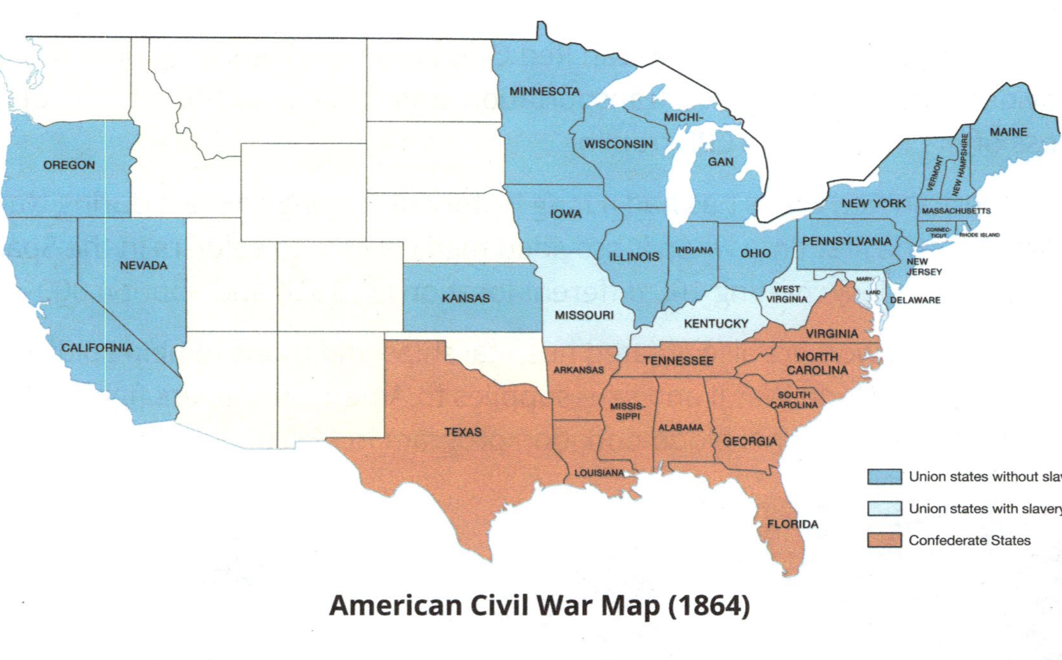

American Civil War Map (1864)

Two months later, the Battle of Gettysburg occurred in July of 1863 in the town of Gettysburg, Pennsylvania. The three-day battle was a turning point in the Civil War. At first there were more Confederate soldiers than Union soldiers, but this changed. It was also the deadliest battle and weakened the Confederates. As many as 40,000 Yankee and Confederate soldiers died. **Yankee** is a nickname for a person born or living in the northern United States. The Battles of Vicksburg and Gettysburg eventually led to Union victory and the end of slavery in 1865.

What was the importance of the Battles of Vicksburg and Gettysburg?

READ

General Sherman's March to Sea

Near the end of the Civil War, the Union designed a new strategy to defeat the Confederates. This new strategy was used during Sherman's March to Sea, a battle led by General William Tecumseh Sherman between November 12, 1864 and December 22, 1864. Sherman's March to Sea was about 285 miles long. It stretched from Atlanta to the Confederate coastal town of Savannah. The objective of the new strategy, called *total war*, was to prevent Confederate soldiers and civilians from creating militaries. Sherman's army burned down Confederate businesses, civilian homes, and military supplies. They also destroyed crops and took livestock, such as horses and cows. This strategy was very successful, because it not only targeted soldiers but also civilians. Without resources to travel for war and maintain an economy, the power of the Confederates grew significantly weaker.

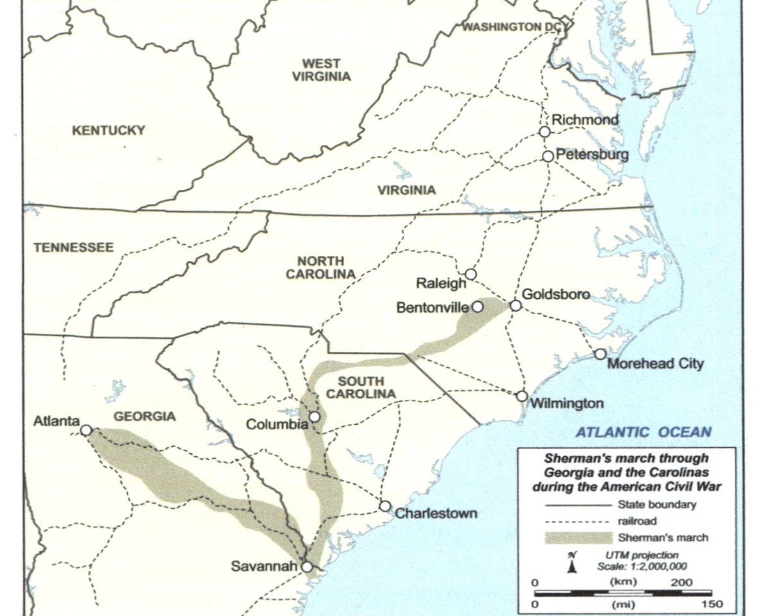

Shermans march through Georgia and the Carolinas map-en.svg by Eric Gaba is in the public domain.

WRITE

What was General Sherman's wartime strategy, and why was it successful?

REVIEW

In this lesson, you learned:

- The American Red Cross provides life-saving humanitarian aid to people in distress.
- During World War I and II, the Red Cross helped injured soldiers, recruited thousands of nurses, and sent supplies to American soldiers who fought in Europe.
- The Union captured and controlled the Mississippi River during the Battle of Vicksburg.
- The Battle of Gettysburg was a turning point in the Civil War.
- During General Sherman's March to Sea, the Union designed and used a new strategy called *total war*.

Think About It

How do you think American life would be different today if the Confederates won the Civil War?

PRACTICE

Use what you know about the American Red Cross and important battles and strategies during the Civil War to complete the table below.

KEY EVENTS AND ORGANIZATIONS	FEATURES	IMPACT ON SOCIETY
American Red Cross		
Battle of Vicksburg		
Battle of Gettysburg		
General Sherman's March		

SHOW WHAT YOU KNOW

Circle True or False.

1. True or False — The American Red Cross provides humanitarian aid such as food, water, shelter, and first aid training for people in distress.

2. True or False — During the Battle of Vicksburg, Union states captured and controlled the Missouri River.

3. True or False — The Battle of Gettysburg was a turning point in the Civil War because the number of Confederates soldiers was greater than Union soldiers.

Circle the correct answer.

4. How did the American Red Cross help soldiers during wars? Circle all that apply.
   - **A.** It recruited thousands of nurses.
   - **B.** It created hospital ships and trains.
   - **C.** It sent supplies to Europe.
   - **D.** It gave people rewards for donating blood.

5. Why was the capture of the Mississippi River a big victory for the Union? Circle all that apply.
   - **A.** The Confederates were cut off from receiving war supplies.
   - **B.** It created more Union states.
   - **C.** It isolated Confederate states such as Texas and Louisiana.
   - **D.** It recruited more soldiers to fight for the Union.

ONLINE CONNECTION

For this activity, create a foldable book to highlight the differences between the Union and the Confederacy. Using an online search engine, research and draw the flags of the Union and Confederacy in your foldable book. Write down different key features between both nations, including their economies, governments, ways of life, outlook on slavery, nicknames, and important battles. Share your book with your instructor.

6. What was the name of the new strategy used by the Union in General Sherman's March to the Sea?
   - **A.** complete war
   - **B.** crushed war
   - **C.** absolute war
   - **D.** total war

7. Which of the following did General Sherman's army not do?
   - **A.** burned down Confederate businesses
   - **B.** killed Confederate leaders
   - **C.** destroyed people's homes
   - **D.** took livestock

Lesson 70

The End of the Civil War

By the end of this lesson, you will be able to:

- identify the main events that resulted in General Lee surrendering his forces
- describe the main points of Lincoln's plan to bring peace to the North and South
- identify the effects that the assassination of Lincoln had on the country

Lesson Review

If you need to review Civil War battles, please go to the lesson titled "Battles and Strategies."

Academic Vocabulary

Read the following vocabulary words and definitions. Look through the lesson. Can you find each vocabulary word? Underline the vocabulary word in your lesson. Write the page number of where you found each word in the blanks.

- **pardon:** the act of freeing a person from punishment for a crime (page ____)
- **racial equality:** the belief that equal opportunities should be given to people of all races (page ____)
- **uprising:** the act of disobeying rules or fighting against authority (page ____)
- **war zone:** an area where a war or wars are being fought (page ____)

Do you know about the national holiday Juneteenth? Juneteenth is short for June 19th. It refers to the day that 250,000 African Americans in Galveston, Texas found out that they had been freed from slavery. The holiday celebrates the Emancipation Proclamation, an order issued by President Abraham Lincoln that began the process of freeing slaves in the United States.

Using an online search engine, research how people celebrate Juneteenth. Present your findings by creating an infographic or a visual representation of your data. You may include the type of music people play, what they eat, and how Juneteenth became a holiday.

EXPLRE

How long is "fourscore and seven years"? On the afternoon of Thursday, November 19, 1863, President Abraham Lincoln delivered a famous speech known as the Gettysburg Address. Lincoln spoke of how humans were equal, as stated in the Declaration of Independence. He also said that the Civil War was a fight not simply for the Union but "a new birth of freedom" that would make everyone truly equal under one united nation.

Lincoln famously began by saying, "fourscore and seven years ago," which refers to the American Revolution of 1776. *Score* is an old word meaning "twenty," so fourscore and seven years means 87 years ago. Lincoln used the ceremony at Gettysburg to encourage people to help America's democracy so that the "government of the people, by the people, for the people, shall not perish (be destroyed) from the earth."

President Lincoln's Gettysburg Address

People meeting in Gettysburg to hear Lincoln's speech.

President Lincoln's speech was one of the many important events during the Civil War. Why do you think his Gettysburg Address was so powerful? Write your ideas on the lines below.

....

....

....

....

....

READ

The End of the Civil War

You learned in the previous lesson that near the end of the Civil War, the Union designed a new strategy to defeat the Confederates. This strategy was called *total war* and was used during General Sherman's March to the Sea in 1864. Total war prevented Confederate soldiers and civilians from creating militaries, which weakened the Confederacy.

While the Confederates fought back, they ultimately surrendered to the Union in 1865 for three major reasons. The first reason was the Union's stopping of Confederate troops. Before their surrender, General Robert E. Lee, who was leading the Confederacy, had hoped to unite with additional Confederate troops in North Carolina. He wanted to have enough men and supplies to continue to fight. However, the Union Army shattered that idea when they went through Virginia and stopped the Confederate troops. This forced General Lee and his troops to abandon and retreat from Richmond, the capital of Virginia. The second reason was that the Confederates were low on troops and supplies. Many Confederate soldiers were killed in the war, and supplies were either overused or destroyed by the Union. The third reason is most troops began to desert their **war zones**, believing that they could not defeat the Union Army. As a result, General Lee surrendered to the Union leader General Ulysses S. Grant on April 9, 1865, in Appomattox, Virginia. This officially ended the American Civil War.

Statue of General Robert E. Lee

WRITE

Name and describe two reasons that General Lee surrendered to the Union.

READ

Uniting of the North and South

During the Civil War, many Southern states were destroyed. Farms and plantations were burned down, and crops were damaged. Confederate money was now worthless due to the fall of the Confederacy. It was clear that the South needed to be rebuilt. The rebuilding of the South after the Civil War was called the Reconstruction era, which lasted from 1865 to 1877. The purpose of the Reconstruction was to help the South become part of the Union again. Union troops occupied much of the South during the Reconstruction to ensure that laws were followed and that another **uprising**—or act of disobeying rules or fighting against authority—did not occur.

Union (left) and Confederate (right) soldiers.

While many people in the North wanted the South to be punished for leaving the Union, others wanted to forgive them and reunite the country as one nation. This included President Abraham Lincoln, who wanted to be lenient to the South. To do this, President Lincoln proposed that any Southerner who took an oath to the Union would be given a **pardon**, or freeing a person from punishment for a crime. He also stated that if 10 percent of Confederate voters supported the Union, which included making slavery illegal, then that state could be readmitted.

In addition, President Lincoln and General Grant were generous to the Confederates so long as they agreed to the terms of peace. These terms included Confederate soldiers turning in rifles in exchange for keeping their horses and mules. Many Southerners, including General Lee, accepted these terms, feeling that they were fair rules.

WRITE

Describe President Lincoln's plan for reuniting the North and South.

Effects of Lincoln's Assassination

On the evening of April 14, 1865, just five days after the end of the Civil War, President Lincoln was assassinated by a Confederate named John Wilkes Booth. Lincoln's Reconstruction plans were never implemented. When Vice President Andrew Johnson became president, he was more lenient to the South. He let Southern states form new governments. Southerners did not like that slavery was illegal after the Civil War, so they created the Black Codes. The Black Codes were laws that prevented African Americans from voting, attending school, and owning land. These laws were not abolished until the Civil Rights Act of 1964.

John Wilkes Booth

The effects of President Lincoln's death and President Johnson's Reconstruction plans marked the beginning of the fight for **racial equality** among African Americans. To protect the rights of all citizens, three amendments were added to the US Constitution:

- The Thirteenth Amendment abolished slavery.
- The Fourteenth Amendment made African Americans citizens of the United States and stated that all people were protected equally by the law.
- The Fifteenth Amendment gave all male citizens the right to vote regardless of race.

How did Lincoln's assassination affect society?

In this lesson, you learned:

- The Confederates surrendered because the Union stopped Confederate troops, they were running out of soldiers and supplies, and they were deserting their war zones.
- The Reconstruction's purpose was to reunite the South with the Union.
- After President Lincoln's death, the Black Codes were created by Southern leaders to restrict African American freedoms.
- The Thirteenth, Fourteenth, and Fifteenth Amendments were added to the US Constitution to protect the rights of people.

Think About It

How do you think the Reconstruction era would have been different if President Lincoln was not assassinated?

PRACTICE

Use what you know about the major events of the Civil War to complete the table below.

KEY EVENTS AND ORGANIZATIONS	FEATURES	IMPACT ON SOCIETY
General Lee's Surrender to the Union		
The Reconstruction Era		
President Lincoln's Assassination		

Use the words in the Word Bank to complete the sentences.

Word Bank: General Lee President Lincoln Reconstruction uprising

1. ______________ proposed that any Southerner who took an oath to the Union would be given a pardon.
2. The ______________ was a period after the Civil War to help the South become a part of the Union again.
3. Union leaders feared an ______________, so they sent troops to occupy the South after the Civil War.
4. ______________ had hoped to unite with additional Confederate troops in North Carolina.Circle the correct answer.

Imagine not being able to attend school due to your skin color. How would you feel? After the Civil War, discrimination against African Americans continued. New laws were created, which kept African Americans separate from white people.

Using an online search engine, look for at least three photos showing different laws during the Jim Crow era (1870s–1950s). Create a photo collage and write a short caption that best describes what is happening in each photo, including how you think people felt. Share and discuss your collage with your instructor.

Circle the correct answer.

5. Which of the following was not a reason for General Lee's surrender to the Union?

A. The Confederates were low on supplies.

B. The Confederate troops were deserting their war zones.

C. The Union halted Confederate troops.

D. Confederate troops wanted to join the Union.

6. What were some of the goals of the Reconstruction era? Circle all correct answers.

A. to help the South become part of the Union again

B. to rebuild the South

C. to make slavery legal again

D. to prevent another uprising in the South

7. What were the Black Codes?

A. laws that restricted the freedoms of African Americans

B. laws that prevented the Confederates from entering Union states

C. laws that kept the Union Army from entering Confederate states

D. laws that abolished slavery after the Civil War

Lesson 71

Chapter 11 Review

In this lesson, you will:

- review the information from the lessons in Chapter 11, "The Civil War."

Lesson Review

Throughout the chapter, we have learned the following big ideas:

- Seven states seceded from the United States and formed their own government known as the Confederate States of America. (Lesson 63)
- The Battle of Fort Sumter signaled the start of the American Civil War. (Lesson 64)
- The Civil War divided America's strengths and loyalties. (Lesson 65)
- The South's strong leadership nearly brought a quick end to the Civil War. (Lesson 66)
- The Emancipation Proclamation was a document signed by President Abraham Lincoln with the intention of setting slaves free in Confederate states. (Lesson 67)
- There were a number of advancements in weapons, tactics, and strategy in the Civil War. (Lesson 68)
- Key battles shifted the fighting into the Southern states midway through the war. (Lesson 69)
- The assassination of Abraham Lincoln caused turmoil after the Confederate surrender. (Lesson 70)

Go back and review the lessons as needed while you complete the activities.

Create a diorama to highlight the main features in the Emancipation Proclamation. You may include a visual representation of President Lincoln signing the document, where it was signed, what the document stated, the leaders who supported and were against it, and how it impacted American society after the Civil War. You may use any cardboard box and create your model with pictures, figurines, and craft supplies.

Making a Diorama

The Beginnings of The Civil War

In this chapter, we learned about the major events leading up to the Civil War, its battles, and the aftermath. Review these events below.

- Nov. 1860: Lincoln is elected President
- Jan./Feb. 1861: seven slave states secede (South Carolina, Mississippi, Florida, Alabama, Georgia, Louisiana, and Texas)
- Mar. 1861: Lincoln is inaugurated
- Apr. 1861: South Carolina forces took Fort Sumter
- Apr. 1861: Lincoln calls for troops
- May/Jun. 1861: Arkansas, Virginia, Tennessee, and North Carolina secede
- May/Jun. 1861: Fighting begins in Virginia
- Jun. 1861: West Virginia splits from Virginia
- July 1861: The Battle of Bull Run/Washington, D.C. readies for attack

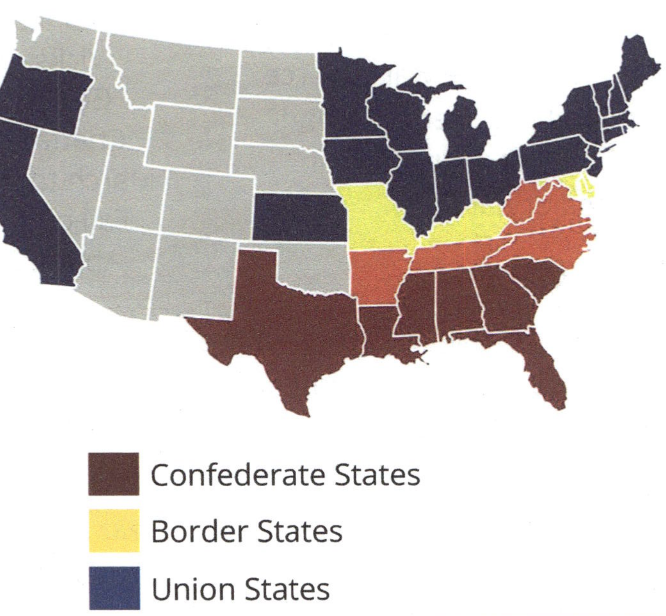

During the war, each side had strengths over the other. For the North, it succeeded the South in its number of states and people, industrial production, and naval power. The North also had an established federal system as well as strong diplomatic ties with Europe. For the South, it succeeded the North in food production and a clear political purpose. In addition, the South had more experienced generals and had quiet support from England.

Why did the Southern states fear Lincoln's election?

Which strength did the North use to effectively cut the South off from trade and resupply?

Strategy and Major Battles

The North developed a strategy early in the war called the Anaconda Plan. The Anaconda Plan called on the Navy to blockade trade to Southern ports and isolate the confederate states. However, the South had no overall strategy. Instead, they attempted to capture Washington, D.C., early in the war to force an end to fighting. When this failed, General Lee tried a second attack through Pennsylvania. After the Battle of Gettysburg in July 1863, the North began to win more major battles.

NORTHERN VICTORIES	SOUTHERN VICTORIES
Antietam, MD 1862	
Fredericksburg, VA 1862	
Shiloh, MS 1862	Bull Run, VA (1st) 1861
Vicksburg, MS 1863	Seven Days, Richmond, VA 1862
Gettysburg, PA 1863	Bull Run, VA (2nd) 1862
Chattanooga, TN 1863	Chancellorsville, VA 1863
March to the Sea, GA 1864	Chickamauga, GA 1863
Fall of Richmond, 1865	
Appomattox, VA 1865	

Slavery Ends and Reconstruction Begins

In the North, former slaves were allowed to serve in the army for the first time as real soldiers, but freedom and equality for all African Americans was slow. First, Lincoln freed the slaves in the confederate states by the Emancipation Proclamation of 1863. It was not until the passage of the 13th Amendment in 1865 that all slavery was banned. The 14th Amendment declared that former slaves were US citizens. The 15th Amendment granted voting rights to African American men.

During the course of the war in the South, the North destroyed both a great deal of property and the South's economic system. Reconstruction was Lincoln's plan to reunite the South and the North. Federal troops were to occupy the South to prevent uprisings. Former confederate soldiers were given pardons so they could resume normal lives. States would be readmitted to the Union after ten percent of the voting population took an oath of allegiance to the United States. After Lincoln's assassination, the reconstruction plan was rapidly dismantled by President Johnson. Johnson, who was from Tennessee, allowed Southern states to create laws called Black Codes that restricted freedom of African Americans.

What advantage did the Northern forces get from winning Vicksburg from the South?

PRACTICE

Read each vocabulary word shown below. Then write a fact or draw a picture for each vocabulary word based on your understanding of the Civil War.

CONFEDERATE STATES OF AMERICA	SECEDE
SABOTAGE	**ANACONDA PLAN**
RATIFY	**AMERICAN RED CROSS**
PARDON	**RACIAL EQUALITY**

PRACTICE

Major Events of the Civil War

Using what you know about the Civil War, write a sentence for each major event below that highlights its importance or significance.

1. The Battle of Fort Sumter

....

....

2. The Battle of Gettysburg

....

....

3. General Sherman's March to the Sea

....

....

4. The Creation of the American Red Cross

....

....

5. The Emancipation Proclamation

....

....

6. The Reconstruction Era

....

....

The Civil War was the first time humans went to war in the air and under the sea. The first submarines were used to block harbors. The North used air balloons to map out enemy positions and direct cannon fire. Probably the most important innovation of the war was the creation of the Army Ambulance Corps. The men of the corps went onto the battlefield and brought out the wounded men to field hospitals. In previous wars, men depended on friends to help them. The ambulances were horse-drawn carts.

PRACTICE

The Union vs. the Confederacy

Using what you know about the Union and Confederacy, fill in the Venn diagram below. You may include their differences in ideas, economy, government, leadership, weaponry, flag design, and armies. If you need help, refer to the worktext, previous lessons, or an online search engine for additional information.

UNION

BOTH

CONFEDERACY

SHOW WHAT YOU KNOW

Think about what you've learned about in this chapter. Circle how you feel:

4 - I know this chapter really well. I could teach it to someone.

3 - I know this chapter pretty well.

2 - I am still learning this chapter. I am not sure about some things.

1 - I am confused. I have a lot of questions about what I've learned.

Talk to your instructor about your answers. When you're ready, ask your instructor for the Show What You Know activity for the chapter.